The Story
of Angels

by Donald F. Ginkel

A study of angels
from the Holy Bible

Additional copies of this book and other Bible studies for young people and adults plus other materials for church growth may be ordered from Church Press, Inc. Ask for a brochure.

CHURCH PRESS, INC.
Rev. Donald F. Ginkel
Toll Free: 1-888-772-8878

Contents

The Story of Angels

Scripture taken from the HOLY BIBLE: NEW INTERNATIONAL VERSION by the International Bible Society. Used by permission of Zondervan Bible Publishers.

Cover Images © 1998 Photo Disc, Inc.

The Story of Angels
Copyrighted © by Donald F. Ginkel, 1998
ISBN 0-9642122-9-3

Printed in the United States of America

THE STORY OF ANGELS

Their Beginning and Being

Opening Hymn

Holy, holy, holy, Lord God Almighty!
Early in the morning our song shall rise to Thee.
Holy, holy, holy, merciful and mighty!
God in three Persons, blessed Trinity.

Holy, holy, holy! All the saints adore Thee,
Casting down their golden crowns around the glassy sea;
Cherubim and seraphim falling down before Thee,
Which were and art and evermore shalt be.

D r. Billy Graham writes, "Have you ever seen or met one of these superior beings called angels? They are God's messengers whose chief business is to carry out His orders in the world. He has given them ambassadorial charge. He has designated and empowered them as holy deputies to perform works of righteousness. In this way they assist Him as their Creator while He sovereignly controls the universe. So He has given them the capacity to bring His holy enterprises to a successful conclusion" (*Angels: God's Secret Agents*, p. 18).

There is a great deal of interest in angels these days in movies, TV, greeting cards, collectibles, boutiques, and books. They are presented to us as cute little cherubs, as aliens from outer space, as neat little friends, and as souls of the dead. A priest named Father Francis makes this interesting observation, "Hollywood and Hallmark have done a terrible injustice to the angelic order. Angels are going to file a class-action lawsuit for misrepresentation."

Recent Gallup polls show that belief in angels has exceeded 70% of our population. Yet, in Acts 23:8 we read, "The Sadducees say that there is no resurrection, and that there are neither *angels* nor spirits, but the Pharisees acknowledge them all." We know that everyone will finally believe in angels — "When the Son of Man comes in His glory, and *all the angels* with Him (Matthew 25:31).

BIBLE STUDY

St. Paul warned the Colossian church: "Do not let anyone who delights in false humility and the *worship of angels* disqualify you for the prize. Such a person goes into great detail about what he has seen, and his unspiritual mind puffs him up with idle notions" (Colossians 2:18). What a significant warning for those who get carried away with their beliefs in angels. So many people seem to base their opinions on observations and experiences. What we believe must be firmly established in Holy Scripture. That is what we will do in this study. We will not do what one confirmation student did. He was asked to list the Ten Commandments in any order. He wrote: "3, 6, 1, 8, 4, 9, 2, 10, 7, 5." We will try to approach the subject of angels in a very orderly way.

Their Creation

Karen Goldman writes:

> "Angels never bother about the mood you may be in, your past, or whether you consider yourself 'spiritual' or not. They see you for what you really are — an angel. And, no matter what, to an angel that is always holy" (*The Angel Book*, p. 50).

> "Whatever an angel has given to you is a gift you are then to give to someone else. And each time the gift changes hands, an angel is born" (*Angel Voices*, p. 97).

1. What is Karen Goldman suggesting to us? _____

    _____

    What is the basis for her beliefs? _____

    Why might it be difficult to dissuade her from her beliefs? _____

One Sunday morning during the childrens' talk I asked a girl what was going to happen to her when she died and went to heaven. She smiled and said, "Oh, then I'll become an angel!" Where do you suppose she got that idea? _____

2. What do we learn from Exodus 20:11 about the creation of angels?

_____

3. Read Psalm 148:2,5. Why are the angels commanded to praise the Lord? _____

4. What does Job 38:4,6-7 tell us about the time of their creation?

_____

Why this extreme happiness on their part? _____

_____

"They were not created before the universe, because before the universe there was only God (John 1:1-2). They were not created after the universe, because after the creation of the universe God "rested from all His work: (Genesis 2:2-3). On which day of the hexaemeron they were created cannot be determined with certainty, because Scripture is silent on this point" (*Christian Dogmatics*, Vol. I, p. 499, Dr. Francis Pieper).

- **BY WHOM**

The angels did not come about by procreation or evolution or the "Big Bang." Angels are creatures. They were created just like you and me at the hand of the Lord. Caroline M. Noel wrote —

> At Jesus' voice creation Sprang at once to sight,
> All the angel faces, All the hosts of light,
> Thrones and dominations, Stars upon their way,
> All the heav'nly orders In their great array.

1. Read John 1:1-3. Who is the Creator of everything including the angels? _____

2. Read Colossians 1:16-17. Jesus is both the means and the purpose of the creation of the angels. What is meant by the "purpose"?

_____

True or False: The words "thrones or powers or rulers or authorities" suggest some order of rank and status.

Which words state that Christ preserves all things? _____

_____ What does that mean? _____

_____

3. Read Revelation 4:11. Why is God worthy of the unending praise

of men and angels? _____

The Greek word for "created" is from the Hebrew word *bara*, which means to call into existence out of nothing. Do you agree that angels do a much better job than we do in praising God for their

creation and preservation? _____ Why is this? _____

_____

- **POSITION CONTRASTED TO THEIR CREATOR**

1. The angels' position to Christ, the Creator, is vast. Hebrews 1 paints a picture of their position. Read 1:4-5. How is Christ, the

Creator, contrasted to the angels in verse 4? _____

What did God never say to any angel according to verse 5? _____

_____

God has, however, called Jesus His "Son" many times in a most exalted sense. Name at least one occasion when God did this.

2. Read Hebrews 1:13. The quote is from Psalm 110 written by David. In that day conquering kings displayed their victory when they placed a foot on the neck of a conquered king. What does God

mean in this quote? _____

The enemies of Jesus will not be annihilated, but they will be subjected. As it applies to angels, what statement is God making

here? _____

Read Hebrews 2:5-9. What does verse 5 tell us in contrast to verse 8b? _____

What does verse 9 tell us about Jesus and angels? _____

_____

3. The Creator stands far apart and above the angels. A. W. Tozar says,

> He is as high above an archangel as above a caterpillar, for the gulf that separates the archangel from the caterpillar is but finite, while the gulf between God and the archangel is infinite. The caterpillar and the archangel, though far removed from each other in the scale of created things, are nevertheless one in that they are alike created. They both belong in the category of that-which-is-not-God and are separated from God by infinitude itself.

Briefly discuss the implications of Tozar's statement.

Purpose of Their Creation

Why are there angels? God doesn't *need* them. He does use them. St. Augustine wrote,

> The Angels are spirits, but it is not because they are spirits that they are Angels. They become Angels when they are sent, for the name Angel refers to their office, not to their nature. You ask the name of this nature, it is spirit; you ask its office, it is that of an Angel (i.e., messenger). In as far as he exists, an Angel is a spirit; in as far as he acts, he is an Angel" (*Sermon on Psalm 103*).

St. Paul writes, "All things were created by Him and *for* Him" (Colossians 1:16b). What does Hebrews 2:10 tell us about the purpose of angels and all of creation? _____

• THEY WORSHIP

Both Testaments abound with references to the activity of angels. One book, however, contains more references to angels than any of the others — Revelation. There they are presented as protecting the saints, administering God's wrath, and, especially, they are portrayed as worshiping the Lamb — the Lord Jesus!

7

Angels seem to have no trouble with worshiping each other; they must know better. They do know how to worship the Lord. From Genesis to Revelation there is a lot of angel worship of the Lord. God actually commands every angel to worship the Son, Jesus Christ. "When God brings His firstborn into the world, *He says*, 'Let all God's angels worship Him'" (Hebrews 1:6)

The prophet Nehemiah says (9:6), "You give life to everything, and the multitudes of heaven *worship* You." Some day our worship will be as pure and real as the angels'. What an experience that will be!

Give a thumb nail sketch of these verses from Revelation:

5:11-12 _____

_____

7:11-12 _____

_____

22:8-9 _____

- **THEY SERVE**

What is specifically mentioned about the duties of angels in these verses:

Deuteronomy 33:3b? _____

Psalm 103:20-21? _____

Hebrews 1:7,14? _____

Their Names

The term "angel" is an official title and is referred to over 300 times in Scripture. In the Old Testament the word used most frequently for "angel" is *malak* which means messenger or representative. The New Testament word for "angel" comes from the Greek *angelos* (αγγελοσ) meaning messenger. The preachers of God's Word are often called angels or messengers (Malachi 2:7; 3:1; Matthew 11:10). Lesson 4 will deal exclusively with the Angel of the Lord, which is the Lord Jesus Christ.

Their Home

The home of the holy angels is God's heaven. When the angels left the shepherds they returned *"into heaven"* (Luke 2:15). In Luke 22:43, "An angel *from heaven* appeared to Him and strengthened Him." Matthew 28:2 says, "An angel of the Lord came down *from heaven* and, going to the tomb, rolled back the stone." Nehemiah 9:6 says, "The multitudes *of heaven* worship You." Jesus teaches us, "For I tell you that their angels *in heaven* always see the face of My Father *in heaven*" (Matthew 18:10). They live in heaven because they belong to God.

Their Properties

"The angels are spirits (πνευματα), that is, immaterial beings. Luke 24:39 forbids us to ascribe to the angels even an ethereal corporeity... The difference between God as spirit (πνευμα) (John 4:24: 'God is a spirit') and the angels as spirits (πνευματα) (Hebrews 1:14: 'Are they not all ministering spirits?') is the difference between God as the Creator and the angels as finite spirits, finite creatures" (*Christian Dogmatics*, Vol. I, pp. 500-501, by Dr. Francis Pieper).

- **APPEARANCE**

How do you picture an angel in your mind? Do you picture a feminine angel with long flowing hair hovering near a child's bed at night? Do you picture a handsome male angel in Jesus' empty tomb? Are they chubby little cupids shooting arrows? Gary Kinnaman writes —

> There are uncanny similarities in my collection of accounts of angel appearances — especially in the descriptions of the angels themselves. They are almost always very tall, usually around ten feet. They are bright, glowing white, often with a slight bluish tint. Their faces are indescribable, so their gender is unrecognizable. They are usually dressed in a full-length robe and frequently girded with a belt or sash of gold. Unless they are appearing as human beings, which seems to be the case in many of the accounts I heard, angels are transparent. Many people told me the angel they saw was "see-through." (*Angels Dark and Light*, p. 52)

How do these verses describe angels:

Matthew 28:3-4? _____

Hebrews 13:2? _____

Revelation 15:6 (Meaning of colors)? _____

Revelation 18:1? _____

What does Acts 6:15 suggest? _____

Do angels have **halos**? The word itself does not even appear in the Bible. Do they play **harps**? We cannot find a single verse that would say this. Do angels have **wings**? Generally, no, even though pictures usually portray them with wings. Isaiah's vision of the Throne of God is one of the exceptions. We will study the seraphim in Lesson 3.

- **HOLY**

Jesus speaks about returning to earth with "the *holy* angels" (Mark 8:38). They were created holy and remained so after the fall. They have not experienced sin and its consequences nor redemption by the blood of God's Son.

- **BRIGHTNESS**

People who see angels, both in Bible times and today, usually describe the angel as having a brilliant light, but a light that is difficult to describe. When an angel appeared to the shepherds at Bethlehem we read that "the *glory* of the Lord shone around them, and they were terrified" (Luke 2:9). The resurrection angels appeared "in clothes that *gleamed like lightning*" (Luke 24:4). When the angel came to get Peter out of his jail we read that "a light *shone* in the cell" (Acts 12:7). In Revelation 10:1 there was an angel "with a rainbow above his head; his face was like the *sun*, and his legs were like *fiery* pillars."

- **ETERNAL**

The angels do not get sick, get old, and finally die like we do. Gabriel appeared to Daniel (Daniel 9) and 500 years later to Zacharias (Luke 1:5-25). He did not appear to have aged. "They can *no longer die*, for they are like the angels" (Luke 20:36).

- **EMOTIONS**

10

When comedian Chris Farley died of a drug overdose at 33 years of age in Chicago, Rev. Miachel Rocha said at Chris' funeral, "You can hear the angels laughing right now because of him." Well, maybe — maybe not. First, there is no word that Chris was a believer in Jesus Christ as his personal Savior. Second, it is very questionable that angels find Chris' humor funny. But angels do have emotions! What do these verses suggest?

Job 38:7 _____

Isaiah 6:3 _____

Luke 15:10 _____

- **SEXLESS**

In Matthew 22:30 Jesus says, "At the resurrection people will neither marry nor be given in marriage; they will be like the angels in heaven." They are not sexual and do not procreate. When seen by humans they usually take the form of a man, and the masculine pronoun is used of them.

- **INNUMERABLE**

In medieval days people used to argue over how many angels could dance on the head of a pin. Idle speculation we say. We are given some information on the shear number of angels. What do these verses suggest?

Deuteronomy 33:2 _____

Daniel 7:10 _____

Revelation 5:11 _____

It is safe to say that their number may be beyond billions. What does the unbelievably large number of angels tell us about God? _____

- **POWERFUL**

1. People who like soft, exquisite angels also seem to like a soft, exquisite God. Angels are not soft or weak, but very powerful. It took only one angel to kill the firstborn in Egypt. David writes,

11

"Praise the Lord, you His angels, you *mighty* ones who do His bidding" (Psalm 103:20). They are mighty, but they are not almighty like God. Their power is astonishing.

2. 2 Thessalonians 1:7 reads, "...when the Lord Jesus is revealed from heaven in blazing fire with His *powerful* angels." The Greek word for "powerful" is δυναμεωσ from which we get the word "dynamite." Angels have explosive power! For us that's a warning and a comfort.

3. Revelation 18:21 reads, "Then a *mighty* angel picked up a boulder the size of a large millstone and threw it into the sea, and said:'With such violence the great city of Babylon will be thrown down, never to be found again.'" While this is a symbolic act, what does it nevertheless suggest about this angel? _____

_____

4. Matthew 28:2 — "There was a violent earthquake, for an angel of the Lord came down from heaven and, going to the tomb, *rolled back the stone* and sat on it." It is estimated that this stone weighed over 8,000 pounds. How much do you think this taxed the angel's resources? _____

Why do you suppose that God made angels so powerful? _____

_____

- **SWIFT**

1. A wife told of this incident: "My husband, a minister, was standing in front of the congregation one morning, about to give the benediction. Dressed in his white robe and with his arms outstretched, he looked just like an angel ready to ascend. I had to squelch laughter when our teenage son leaned over and whispered in my ear, 'He'll never get off the ground.'" No such trouble with real angels!

2. How fast are angels? Light travels at the speed of 186,000 miles per second, so it takes less than a second for light to travel the distance around the earth — less than a second! Angels are faster! Bear in mind that they must move spatially even though they are spirits.

This does not seem to slow them down.

3. Psalm 104:4 — "He makes *winds* his messengers (angels), flames of fire his servants." Daniel 9:21 — "While I was still in prayer, Gabriel, the man I had seen in the earlier vision, came to me in *swift flight* about the time of the evening sacrifice." Why do you think the Lord gave the angels this incredible speed? _____

_____

- **KNOWLEDGEABLE**

1. What does Genesis 24:1-7 tell us about angels? _____

_____

2. In 2 Samuel 14:20 a woman of Tekoah said of King Solomon, "My lord has *wisdom like that of an angel* of God – he knows everything that happens in the land." We believe that angels have great inherited wisdom given them at creation, but they also acquire knowledge. They possess intelligence. They are not omniscient like God. They do not understand everything about salvation but are learning (1 Peter 1:11-12), and they are unaware of the timing of Christ's second coming (Matthew 24:36).

3. True or False: Chances are that angels know a great deal more about us than we known about ourselves.

My wife and I were walking along the bay in Monterey, CA, in the bright sun discussing angels. I said to her, "I just might be an angel in disguise." She quickly responded, "No, no!" I said, "How do you know that?" She said, "Angels are confirmed in their bliss and you are not!"

- **CONFIRMED IN HOLINESS**

1. What do these verses tell us about the holy angels?

1 Timothy 5:21 _____

_____

Luke 20:36a _____

_____

Matthew 18:10b _____

_____

2. The reason for the holy angels election is very different from our election. They were obedient; we have been disobedient. Jesus did not die for them; He did die for us. The holy angels are now incapable of sin. When we get to heaven we, too, will be incapable of sin. All the holy angels and all believers will live eternally in holiness to the glory of our God and Savior! What a great day that will be! Hallelujah!

Concluding Thoughts

1. Why do you suppose angels are so popular today? _____
   _____

2. Where do people seem to get their information on angels? _____
   _____

3. True or False: Baby angels are sometimes called cherubs.

4. Why is it important for today's believer to have a thorough Bible study on angels? _____

5. True or False: Jesus created the angels.

6. Read Psalm 103:20-21. Mention several points about angels from these verses: _____
   _____

7. True or False: I find it difficult to believe that I have experienced what is taught in Hebrews 13:1. In either case, why? _____
   _____

8. True or False: Angels know almost everything. Defend your answer.

9. True or False: Angels in the Old Testament are occasionally presented as women with wings.

10. God could do everything by Himself, but He decided to create and employ angels and believers in His service. Why do you suppose He

did it this way? _____

_____

Closing Prayer

Almighty and everlasting God, we deeply praise You for this first Lesson on *The Story of Angels*. Lord Jesus, we believe that You created the angels and You preserve them. They worship You and serve You and so should we. Their home is heaven and so is ours. They are holy and so are we through Your blood. Their number, their power, their speed, and their knowledge demonstrate Your greatness. We look forward to the day when we go to heaven and we are confirmed in holiness and when we join the angels in giving You perfect praise and serving You with great joy forever and ever. Bless this Bible study unto us. Bless the invitations we extend to others this week to come and join us as we sit at Your feet to learn from You. We pray this with grateful hearts and in Your name! Amen.

Closing Hymn

Holy, holy, holy! Though the darkness hide Thee,
Though the eye made blind by sin Thy glory may not see,
Only Thou art Holy, there is none beside Thee,
Perfect in pow'r, in love and purity.

Holy, holy, holy! Lord God Almighty!
All thy works shall praise Thy name in earth and sky and sea.
Holy, holy, holy, merciful and mighty!
God in three Persons, blessed Trinity!

THE STORY OF ANGELS

Satan and the Fallen Angels

Opening Hymn

A mighty fortress is our God, A trusty shield and weapon;
He helps us free from ev'ry need That hath us now o'ertaken.
The old evil foe Now means deadly woe;
Deep guile and great might Are his dread arms in fight;
On earth is not his equal.

With might of ours can naught be done, Soon were our loss effected;
But for us fights the valiant One, Whom God Himself elected.
Ask ye, Who is this? Jesus Christ it is,
Of sabaoth Lord, And there's none other God;
He holds the field forever.

C. S. Lewis wrote: "There are two equal and opposite errors into which our race can fall about the devils. One is to disbelieve in their existence. The other is to believe and to feel an excessive and unhealthy interest in them. They themselves are equally pleased by both errors and hail a materialist and a magician with the same delight" (*The Screwtape Letters*).

Years ago, when the famous evangelist Billy Sunday was asked, "Do you believe in a real devil?" it is said that he responded, "The Bible declares it to be so, and further, I have done business with him myself." So have you and I.

A recent poll indicates that 75% of Americans believe that angels are real and affect people today. Yet 62% said they do not believe in a real Devil, that Satan is not a living being but is only a symbol of evil.

52% of "Christians" interviewed agreed that Satan is not real. Is the Devil doing a good job or what? It appears that many "Christians" do not know what the Holy Bible teaches about Satan and the evil angels.

Their Origin and Fall

1. Some Jewish thought presents these two scenarios:

> That demons were not to be seen as independent powers in rebellion against God was made clear in several passages from the Talmud and Midrash. According to one passage, as God approached the end of the six days of His Creation, He was engaged in the making of souls, but He stopped as the Sabbath arrived without having supplied bodies to those souls. These "disembodied" souls are demons. Another version explains the origin of demons in the cohabitation of Adam with shady female spirits during his temporary (130 years!) separation from Eve following their expulsion from the Garden of Eden. Out of Adam's extramarital sexual activity, demons by the hundreds were born, all of them bearing the shape of human beings (*A Gathering of Angels*, p. 150, by Morris B. Margolies).

A very devout Christian woman went to a pet store. She saw a parrot which she adored and decided to buy it. The owner said, "Lady, I couldn't sell you that parrot. He was owned by a sailor, and he cusses a blue streak."

But the woman could not be dissuaded. She believed that the parrot, with Christian love and firm discipline, could be retrained. She took the parrot home.

The parrot began cussing and swearing. She warned the parrot that she was going to put him in the freezer for ten minutes to teach him to hold his tongue. When the parrot continued to swear, the woman put the caged parrot in the freezer. After ten minutes she took him out.

The shivering parrot seemed to be remorseful. "Ppplease, lllady," said the parrot. "Wwwould yyyou tttell mmme jjjust ooone ttthing? Wwwhat dddid ttthe tttturkey dddo?"

We're a lot like that parrot, and the Devil is a lot like that turkey. We know what we did, but what did the Devil do to end up where he is today? Let's find out.

- TIME OF THE FALL

While we do not know the specific day of the fall of Satan and his evil angels, two passages give us the time frame. In John 8:44 Jesus says, "The devil... was a murderer from *the beginning*." And in 1 John 3:8, "The devil has been sinning from *the beginning*." Between the creation and his appearance in the Garden, Satan fell. It would appear to be a short period of time.

- ### NATURE OF THE FALL

1. We know that every created thing that was made was made during the six days, including the angels. Genesis 1:31 says, "God saw *all* that He had made, and it was *very good*." Twenty-six verses later we read, "Now the *serpent* was more crafty than any of the wild animals the LORD God had made. He said to the woman..." (Genesis 3:1). Something awesome and terrible had happened. What was it?

   _____

2. How could sin come about in a perfect heaven and perfect earth?

   It seems almost inconceivable that any so highly privileged as to live so near the throne of God, beholding and bathing in His glory, should sin against Him and consequently suffer expulsion from His presence. But such was the case, and Scripture is not silent as to open rebellion in the angelic hierarchy" (*All the Angels in the Bible*, p. 43, Herbert Lockyer).

3. Read Ezekiel 28:11-17. It is felt by some expositors, including Dr. Billy Graham, that these verses not only speak to the King of Tyre in a literal sense, but that there is an allegory to it, namely a description of Lucifer. Why might we conclude that these verses also apply to Lucifer? _____

   _____

   _____

   After reading Ezekiel 28:6, how do you picture Satan? _____

   _____

4. Read Isaiah 14:12-15. This Chapter not only refers to the king of Babylon, but to Lucifer ("morning star" verse 12). The Vulgate translates, "Lucifer, the morning star," and the King James

translates, "Lucifer, son of the morning." In verses 13-14 Lucifer makes five pronouncements. What are they?

a. _____

b. _____

c. _____

d. _____

e. _____

What does Satan really want to be? _____

5. The sin of Satan is despicable. Here are five reasons why.

> (1) There was no previous example; this was the beginning of rebellion against the most high God. (2) He was created beautiful and perfect; he lacked nothing as the greatest of all creatures. (3) His greatest of all intelligence gave him greater light and understanding of the greatness and goodness of the God against whom he sinned. (4) His highest position gave him the privilege of the greatest service to God. (5) In his perfection and holiness, he had the privilege of intimate fellowship with God (*Angels Elect & Evil*), p. 141, C. Fred Dickason).

What are your thoughts at this point? _____

_____

6. Read Revelation 12:7-9. There was a war in heaven. The holy angels were led by Michael and the evil angels were led by Satan. It could be said that Satan is ( ) the opposite of God, ( ) the opposite of Michael, ( ) the opposite of any angel, ( ) none of the above.

7. Remember that in Matthew 22:12 we are told, "Then the king told the attendants, 'Tie him hand and foot, and throw him outside, into the darkness, where there will be weeping and gnashing of teeth.'" The King, Christ, does not evict the evil ones, but has His "attendants," His angels, do so. The dragon is, of course, Satan. The "ancient serpent" in verse 9 harks back to Genesis 3:1 where Satan appeared to Eve. "Devil" comes from διαβολισ, which means "slanderous one, false accuser." John also says the Devil's evil angels were thrown out of heaven with him. Jesus says, "I saw Satan

fall like lightning from heaven" (Luke 10:18). The exodus must have been swift.

What now awaits Satan and all the evil angels? _____

_____

For us, however, God in great mercy has provided a remedy for our sin. Mercy comes to us in the Savior.

From heaven the sinning angels fell,
And wrath and darkness chained them down:
But man, vile man, forsook his bliss,
And mercy lifts him to a crown!

Amazing work of sovereign grace,
That could distinguish rebels so!
Our guilty treasons called aloud
For everlasting fetters too!

To Thee, to Thee, Almighty Love!
Our souls, ourselves, our all we pay!
Millions of tongues shall sound Thy praise,
On the bright hills of heavenly day!

(Author unknown)

- **OTHER NAMES FOR SATAN**

Satan or Lucifer is designated by various names, titles, and descriptions and which reveal his character, such as:

The tempter — Matthew 4:3
The evil one — Matthew 6:13
Beelzebub (lord of the flies), the prince of demons — Matthew 12:24
The enemy — Matthew 13:39
Murderer, a liar, father of lies — John 8:44
Prince of this world — John 12:31
God of this age, blinds minds of unbelievers — 2 Corinthians 4:4
Bilial (worthless one) — 2 Corinthians 6:15
Tormentor — 2 Corinthians 12:7
Ruler of the kingdom of the air — Ephesians 2:2
A roaring lion — 1 Peter 5:8
Angel of the Abyss, Abaddon & Apollyon (destroyer) — Revelation 9:11
Great dragon, ancient serpent, leads world astray — Revelation 12:9
The deceiver — Revelation 20:10

21

What warnings are there for us in these names and titles? _____

_____

- FALLEN ANGELS

Read Revelation 12:3-4. "Enormous red dragon" suggests the extreme power of Satan. Remember that angels are frequently called stars in Revelation. It is assumed that approximately a third of the angels in heaven followed Satan which would mean that the number of evil angels is extremely large. They are under Satan's control and willingly serve him. Matthew 12:24 speaks of "Beelzebub, the *prince of demons*." "Demons" in the New Testament is from the Greek "daimon" (δαιμονια) meaning "evil spirit" and also called "devil." Demons are mentioned over 70 times in the New Testament, and they appear most frequently during the ministry of our Lord.

Read Deuteronomy 32:16-17. What was Israel doing when they worshiped idols? _____
Psalm 106:37 adds, "They sacrificed their sons and their daughters *to demons*."

Their Power

1. How do Satan and the evil angels demonstrate their power according to these verses?

    a. Mark 5:2-9 _____

    b. Mark 9:17-18 _____

    c. 1 Thessalonians 2:18 _____

    d. 2 Thessalonians 2:9 _____

2. What interesting thing do you notice about demon power in these verses?

    a. Job 2:6-7 _____

    b. Exodus 7:10-12 _____

22

c. Luke 4:5-13 _____

3. Most people, in and out of the church, do not seem to appreciate the power of demons. Why? _____

Their Knowledge

What do the following verses tell us about the knowledge of demons?

1. Luke 4:34 _____

2. 2 Corinthians 2:11 _____

3. James 2:19 _____

True or False: Chances are that Satan knows a lot more about you than you do.

On The Attack

An atheist group received permission to place a sign next to a Christmas tree in the capitol of Wisconsin. The sign said, "In this season of Winter Solstice, may reason prevail. There are no gods, no devils, no angels, no heaven or hell. Religion is but a myth that hardens hearts and enslaves minds." A small message written on the back of the sign said, "Thou shalt not steal." Satan and the evil angels are alive and very active, both openly and quietly.

Here are just three verses that describe the attack mode of Satan and his evil angels. "The LORD said to Satan, 'Where have you come from?' Satan answered the LORD,' 'From roaming through the earth and *going back and forth* in it'" (Job 1:7). "Jesus *rebuked Peter. 'Get behind me, Satan!'* He said. 'You do not have in mind the things of God, but the things of men'" (Mark 8:33). "Your enemy the devil *prowls* around like a *roaring lion* looking for someone to *devour*" (1 Peter 5:8).

- A TEMPTER, MURDER AND LIAR

Satan shows his colors in his appearance to Eve in the Garden. In Genesis 3:1-5 he said to Eve, "Did God *really say*, 'You must not eat from any tree in the garden'?... 'You *will not surely die*,' the serpent said to the woman. 'For God knows that when you eat of it your eyes will be opened, and *you will be like God*, knowing good and evil.'" The tempting

23

and lying are obvious. In Matthew 4:3, "The *tempter* came to Him and said, '*If* you are the Son of God, tell these stones to become bread.'" In John 8:44 Jesus paints this portrait of the Devil: "The devil was a *murderer* from the beginning, *not holding to the truth*, for there is *no truth in* him. When he *lies*, he speaks his native language, for *he is a liar* and the *father of lies*." Satan is accused of bringing death to the entire human race, and he did it by lying. Think about that the next time you are tempted to lie.

- ### OPPOSES CHRIST AND HIS CHURCH

Read Luke 4:5-7. Satan acted as if He were

_____. It took Satan just an _____

to let Jesus see every kingdom in the world. Satan could do this because he

possesses great _____. What did

Satan offer to give the Lord? _____

_____

Why did the Devil say he could do this? _____
Satan is suggesting that it is not necessary for the Lord to go to Calvary to suffer agony and death. He need only prostrate Himself before Satan in worship. But the amazing proposal is false and full of lies. The hand-over is a delusion. Jesus would become an enemy of God. All mankind would be eternally lost. What have you learned about Satan here?

_____

- ### OPPOSES BELIEVERS

Read each verse and briefly share the awareness which we should have.

Matthew 24:24 For false Christs and false prophets will appear and perform great signs and miracles to deceive even the elect — if that were possible.

2 Corinthians 2:11 In order that Satan might not outwit us. For we are not unaware of his schemes.

2 Corinthians 11:14 And no wonder, for Satan himself masquerades as an angel of light.

24

2 Corinthians 12:7 To keep me from becoming conceited because of these surpassingly great revelations, there was given me a thorn in my flesh, a messenger of Satan, to torment me.

Ephesians 6:12 For our struggle is not against flesh and blood, but against the rulers, against the authorities, against the powers of this dark world and against the spiritual forces of evil in the heavenly realms.

1 Timothy 4:1 The Spirit clearly says that in later times some will abandon the faith and follow deceiving spirits and things taught by demons.

1 Peter 5:8 Be self-controlled and alert. Your enemy the devil prowls around like a roaring lion looking for someone to devour.

1. What do you suppose is the easiest way for the Devil to deceive you?

_____

2. It is said that one day Martin Luther became so angry over a confrontation with the Devil in his office that he hurled at inkwell at him. Why would he do that? _____

● **IN RELATION TO UNBELIEVERS**

Read each verse and briefly describe the activity of the Devil and his evil angels.

1 Samuel 16:14 Now the Spirit of the LORD had departed from Saul, and an evil spirit from the LORD tormented him.

Matthew 13:38-39 The field is the world, and the good seed stands for the sons of the kingdom. The weeds are the sons of the evil one, and the enemy who sows them is the devil.

Luke 8:12 Those along the path are the ones who hear, and then the devil comes and takes away the word from their hearts, so that they may not believe and be saved.

2 Corinthians 4:4 The god of this age has blinded the minds of unbelievers, so that they cannot see the light of the Gospel of the glory of Christ.

Ephesians 2:1-2 As for you, you were dead in your transgressions and sins, in which you used to live when you followed the ways of this world and of the ruler of the kingdom of the air, the spirit who is now at work in those who are disobedient.

2 Thessalonians 2:9-10 The coming of the lawless one will be in accordance with the work of Satan displayed in all kinds of counterfeit miracles, signs and wonders, and in every sort of evil that deceives those who are perishing.

In view of this devastating activity by the evil ones, what chance does an unbeliever have of ever being converted and then remaining in saving faith? _____

_____

Their Defeat

The disaster and defeat of the evil spirits is total and complete. How did it occur? "The reason the Son of God appeared was to *destroy* the devil's work" (1 John 3:8). Christ cried, "It is finished!" Then He rose from the dead in great power. The Lord assured the disciples, "The prince of this world now stands *condemned*" (John 16:11). That condemnation is fixed and forever irrevocable. Peter writes (2 Peter 2:4), "God did not spare the angels when they sinned, but sent them to hell, putting them into gloomy dungeons to be *held for judgment.*" "The angels who did not keep their positions of authority but abandoned their own home — these He has *kept in darkness, bound with everlasting chains* for judgment on the great Day" (Jude 6). "Then He will say to those on His left, 'Depart from Me, you who are cursed, *into the eternal fire prepared for the devil and his angels*'" (Matthew 25:41).

● CHRIST IS "THE GREAT EXORCIST"

What activity and purpose do you see taking place between demons and Jesus in these verses?

Matthew 4:24 News about Him spread all over Syria, and people brought to Him all who were ill with various diseases, those suffering severe pain, the demon-possessed, those having seizures, and the paralyzed, and He healed them.

Matthew 17:15,18, "He has seizures and is suffering greatly. He often falls into the fire or into the water..." Jesus rebuked the demon, and it came out of the boy, and he was healed from that moment.

26

Mark 1:32, 34, That evening after sunset the people brought to Jesus all the sick and demon-possessed... and Jesus healed many who had various diseases. He also drove out many demons, but He would not let the demons speak because they knew who He was.

Mark 9:25-26 Jesus rebuked the evil spirit. "You deaf and mute spirit," He said, "I command you, come out of him and never enter him again." The spirit shrieked, convulsed him violently and came out. The boy looked so much like a corpse that many said, "He's dead."

Luke 4:35,36 "Be quiet!" Jesus said sternly. "Come out of him!" Then the demon threw the man down before them all and came out without injuring him. All the people were amazed and said to each other, "What is this teaching? With authority and power He gives orders to evil spirits and they come out!"

Luke 8:2 ... and also some women who had been cured of evil spirits and diseases: Mary (called Magdalene) from whom seven demons had come out.

- **CHRIST IS OUR VICTORY**

Someone said that if Satan cannot get us to sin, then he'll accuse us of sin. Well put. Sometimes he does both. First Satan tempted Judas to sin, and then he accused him of his sin. But still we win. Jesus is stronger than Satan. Jesus is all-knowing, all-wise, all holy, and God Almighty! The Devil is none of these.

1. In precise terms, how did Jesus defeat the Devil according to Hebrews 2:14-15? _____

   _____

2. What should you remind yourself of on a daily basis according to 1 John 4:4? _____

3. Read 1 John 5:18. What's the good news every day? _____

   _____

4. How does Romans 8:38-39 put it? _____

27

Dr. Robert M. M'Cheyne speaks for all of us:

> When I stand before the throne
> Dressed in beauty not my own,
> When I see Thee as Thou art,
> Love Thee with unsinning heart;
> Then, Lord, shall I fully know —
> Not till then — how much I owe.

Concluding Thoughts

1. Do you believe in the reality of the Devil too much or not enough? _____ Why? _____
What is the danger of going to either extreme? _____
_____

2. Why do you suppose there are so many misconceptions of Satan and the evil angels? _____

3. Many people say that they believe in God and in angels, but they do not believe in a real Devil. How come? _____
_____

4. How well can the Devil quote Scripture and how does this thought affect you? _____
_____

5. How might Satan as an "angel of light" go about misleading Christians? _____
_____

6. The sin of insatiable pride proved to be Satan's downfall. Why must we be very careful about the sin of pride in our lives? _____
_____

7. True or False: It is perfectly harmless for children to dress up like the Devil on Halloween. Defend your answer. _____

_____

_____

8. If you could ask Satan one question, what would it be? _____

_____

9. What advice do these verses have for us?

   a. Proverbs 16:18 _____

   _____

   b. Romans 12:3 _____

   _____

10. What encouragement do you find in John 17:15? _____

   _____

   In John 17:17? _____

   _____

Closing Prayer

O Lord our God, thanks be to You for giving us details on the fall of Satan and the evil angels. It is inconceivable that anyone as privileged as Satan was before the fall should turn against You. You created him beautiful and perfect and gave him great intelligence. He enjoyed intimate fellowship with You. While there is no salvation for fallen angels, You have, in great mercy, provided a remedy for our sin. Only in heaven will we truly appreciate the value of Your sacrifice on the cross. Teach us to be keenly aware of the wicked plans of the evil spirits. We pray that You will empower us by the Holy Spirit to be on our guard and to fight against all of Satan's lying and deceiving. Help us to study our Bibles and to memorize many passages so that we can use them effectively against him. Finally, receive us to Yourself in heaven where there will be no more temptation to sin. There we shall, with angels and archangels and all the saints of heaven, sing praise to Your glory forever and ever. We pray in Your powerful name! Amen.

Closing Hymn

Though devils all the world should fill, All eager to devour us,
We tremble not, we fear no ill, They shall not overpow'r us.
This world's prince may still Scowl fierce as he will,
He can harm us none, He's judged; the deed is done;
One little word can fell him.

The Word they still shall let remain Nor any thanks have for it;
He's by our side upon the plain With His good gifts and Spirit.
And take they our life, Goods, fame, child, and wife,
Though all these be gone, Our vict'ry has been won;
The Kingdom ours remaineth.

THE STORY OF ANGELS

Angel Titles, Names and Activities

Opening Hymn

Ye watchers and ye holy ones,
Bright seraphs, cherubims, and thrones,
Raise the glad strain, Alleluia!
Cry out, dominions, princedoms, pow'rs,
Virtues, archangels, angels' choirs,
Alleluia! Alleluia! Alleluia! Alleluia! Alleluia!

O higher than the cherubim,
More glorious than the seraphim,
Lead their praises, Alleluia!
Thou Bearer of th' eternal Word,
Most gracious, magnify the Lord,
Alleluia! Alleluia! Alleluia! Alleluia! Alleluia!

What do angels do? What is their purpose? Here is non-Biblical view from Terry Lynn Taylor:

Most of all, the angels want to encourage you to have fun, be wild, laugh, frolic, be courageous, and create spontaneity. The angels are right here right now, waiting to have some fun with you. Look up and give them an affirmative nod to let them know you acknowledge their loving presence" (*Creating With the Angels*, p. 4).

Who They Are

The preacher, hoping to get acquainted with one of the new members of the congregation, knocked on the front door of her home one evening. "Is that you, angel?" came the woman's voice from within. "No," replied the minister, "but I'm from the same department." Well, maybe, but only in a very broad sense.

One of the more interesting aspects of the study of angels concerns their ranks or classes. Down through the years people have studied the holy angels and have sometimes concluded that there are three rankings of angels in this order:

Highest Rank: Seraphim, Cherubim, Thrones
Middle Rank: Dominions, Virtues, Powers
Lower Rank: Principalities, Archangels, Angels

While the Bible speaks about ranks and differences in angels, there is not enough evidence to speak in specifics. Most Bible scholars reject specific classes or levels of angels. It is obvious that the angels are organized in some way so that they can execute God's will. The names, titles, and activities of angels lend credence to various groups and levels of angels, but Scripture is silent on the details. We will briefly examine what the Bible does say.

- THRONES, DOMINIONS, PRINCIPALITIES, POWERS

1. Read Ephesians 6:12 carefully. Paul says that our struggle (fight and combat) is not against flesh and blood which we can see, but against a world-wide cast of evil spirits on all levels including the supernatural and transcendental world, but not heaven itself. Every demon has a particular rule or assignment with Satan, the prince of this world, as his head. Just as holy angels have ranks and orders, so also the evil angels (perhaps a carry over from before the fall into sin). This empire of darkness is worldwide. Their war is conducted to bring us into their kingdom and to effect our eternal ruin.

2. Read Colossians 1:16 carefully. Here the spirit world is specifically mentioned in detail: invisible, thrones, powers, rulers, authorities. We cannot see them. These four terms do not designate specific classes or ranks, and, yet, they are there. The spirit world would

not function well without these ranks and authorities.

3. Read Colossians 2:15. Paul is again referring to the ranks of fallen angels (powers and authorities) who held the world in captivity. By His death on the cross Jesus took away their ruling and authoritative power and rescued the fallen human race.

4. These references (thrones, dominions, principalities, powers) apparently apply to both the holy and evil spirits. The fact that holy angels have certain areas of responsibility will be borne out as we continue to study their names and activities.

● ANGELS

"Angel" comes from the Greek word *angelos* (ανγελοσ) and means messenger. In the Old Testament the word used most frequently for angels is *malak* and means messenger or representative. The word "angel" or "angels" is used over 300 times in Scripture.

● HOST

In Luke 2:13 we read, "Suddenly a great company of heavenly *host* appeared with the angel." The Greek word for "host" is *stratias* (στρατιασ). Host as used in both Testaments means an army, a well-trained army, one that is prepared for war, to do God's will and fight His battles. David used the word "host" when he said to Goliath, "I come against you in the name of the LORD Almighty, the God of the *armies* of Israel, whom you have defied" (1 Samuel 17:45). God is pictured as the sovereign commander of a huge heavenly army of holy angels who do His will in heaven and on earth.

What comfort is there for you when you think of "host"? _____

_____

● HOLY ONES

In Deuteronomy 33:2 Moses said, "The Lord came... with myriads of *holy ones.*" Psalm 89:7 says, "In the council of the *holy ones* God is greatly feared." Nebuchadnezzar said, "I looked, and there before me was a messenger, a *holy one,* coming down from heaven... 'The decision is announced by messengers, the *holy ones* declare the verdict'" (Daniel

4:13,17). The nature of these angels is holiness like their God in whose presence they live. They are in constant readiness to serve Jehovah.

Jude 14-15 "Enoch... prophesied about these men: 'See, the Lord is coming with thousands upon thousands of His *holy ones* to judge everyone.'" They are called holy because they are holy. Their holiness comes from God and points to God. They are the separated angels set apart to serve God. Their character and activities show their holiness.

- **ELECT**

St. Paul writes, "I charge you, in the sight of God and Christ Jesus and the *elect angels*" (1 Timothy 5:21). Like all believers, the holy angels have been elected to be with God forever, but not because of what Christ did for them at Calvary. The Bible does not define their election. The evil angels were rejected solely because of their apostasy.

- **MIGHTY ONES**

Psalm 29:1, "Ascribe to the LORD, O *mighty ones*, ascribe to the LORD glory and strength." Psalm 103:20, "Praise the LORD, you His angels, you *mighty ones* who do His bidding, who obey His word." Revelation 10:1-2, "Then I saw another *mighty angel* coming down from heaven. He was robed in a cloud, with a rainbow above his head; his face was like the sun, and his legs were like fiery pillars. He was holding a little scroll, which lay open in his hand. He planted his right foot on the sea and his left foot on the land." Revelation 18:21, "Then a *mighty angel* picked up a boulder the size of a large millstone and threw it into the sea..." They are strong by their appearance and their actions. While

they are mighty, what character of God do angels lack? _____

- **OTHER NAMES**

Psalm 8:5 "You made him (man) a little lower than the *heavenly beings* and crowned him with glory and honor." Psalm 68:17 "The *chariots* of God are tens of thousands and thousands of thousands." Hebrews 1:14 "Are not all angels *ministering spirits* sent to serve those who will inherit salvation?" What is your first name and what does it mean? Mine is Donald. What does it mean? Don't say "duck." The names ascribed to to the angels describe them. What do the italicized words tell us about

angels? _____

Archangel will be studied next.

Michael

1. The word *archangel* means "ruling or chief angel." "Michael" means "who is like God?" What is the answer? _____

2. While Scripture designates only Michael as an archangel (Jude 9), we have Biblical grounds for believing that before his fall Lucifer was also an archangel, equal or perhaps superior to Michael. The prefix "arch" suggests a chief, principal or great angel. Thus, Michael is now the angel above all angels, recognized in rank to be the first prince of heaven. He is, as it were, the Prime Minister in God's administration of the universe, and is the "angel administrator" of God for judgment. He must stand alone, because the Bible never speaks of archangels, only *the* archangel (*Angels God's Secret Agents*, pp. 50,51, Billy Graham).

**Michael —
the warrior
and
protector**

3. Michael is the protector and warrior for God's people — Israel. Daniel 10:13, "Michael, one of the chief princes, came to *help* me." Daniel 12:1, "At that time Michael, the great prince who *protects* your people, will arise."

4. Read Jude 9 very carefully. The Lord buried the body of Moses. It may be that Satan wanted to claim Moses' body for physical decay, and the Lord wanted it preserved from decay. We do not know for sure. We do, however, have an open confrontation between the archangel and the arch fiend!

   True or False: When the Devil claimed Moses' body, Michael rebuked him. Defend your answer: _____

   _____

   Why would Michael not judge the Devil? _____

5. Read 1 Thessalonians 4:16 carefully. What two things will the living and the dead hear on the Last Day? _____

6. Some people speak about Gabriel blowing his trumpet on this day, but not so. The greatest of all the holy angels will speak, and the greatest of all the angels will sound forth the trumpet in connection with the Lord's command. Are

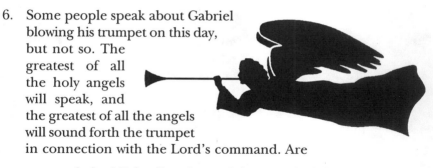

you ready for Michael's voice and the sound of the trumpet? ____

What will your eyes be focused on? _____

Gabriel

1. Can you pick out the truth from the errors in the following?

> Gabriel is associated with a trumpet, symbolizing the voice of God. Gabriel is a bringer of good news and a maker of changes. Gabriel has been credited with announcing the birth of Christ to Mary; with being the guardian of the prophet Muhammad in the Muslim tradition; with being the angel who inspired Joan of Arc to help the king of France; and with influencing Zoroaster. Gabriel announced to qualified human beings the major duties of their spiritual commission for the benefit of the earth. If Gabriel has not spoken or appeared to you to clarify your spiritual gifts, try tuning into his essence. Gabriel has many angels under his influence whom we can tune into for guidance and messages regarding the special part we play in the big picture. So allow messages to come through to inspire you; you may even hear the faint or blasting sound of a trumpet as you receive your messages from God (*Guardians of Hope*, p. 163, Terry Lynn Taylor).

2. Now to what the Bible teaches about Gabriel. His name means "Mighty one of God." He is never called an archangel. It is assumed he is a ruling angel. We read about him four times, and he is always the bringer of good news.

3. Read Daniel 8:16-27 and 9:20-27. What do you learn about Gabriel from these two sections? _____

_____

_____

4. Read Luke 1:19-20. What do you learn about Gabriel here? _____

_____

_____

5. Gabriel's most important message, however, goes to the Virgin Mary about Jesus, God's Son. Read Luke 1:26-38. Describe his activity: _____

_____

_____

Cherubim

1. The first appearance of the Cherubim is in Genesis 3:24. Read it and describe their duty and power: _____

_____

2. Read Ezekiel 1:1-28. What are these creatures (Read Ezekiel 10)?

_____

> Cherubim (Heb. pl. of *cherub*) seem to be angel beings of the highest order or class, created with indescribable powers and beauty. As is the case with many heavenly realities, their character and appearance are so far beyond human imagination and present comprehension that they must be described in earthly terms obviously designed to convey something surpassingly supernatural (Ezekiel 1:5-14; 28:12-13,17) (*Angels Elect & Evil*, pp. 64-65, C. Fred Dickason).

3. We go to the tabernacle. How are the cherubim presented in Exodus 25:17-22? _____

37

Placed at either end of the mercy seat, the cherubim represent a new relationship to God in His holiness and life-imparting presence (Exodus 25:18-20; Psalm 80:1). Their outstretched wings touch each other; they gaze one towards another and downwards upon the ark. The position and attitude of the cherubim upon the mercy seat indicate their attendance upon their Creator and our Redeemer. Their gaze downwards upon the ark suggests their contemplation of the sublime mysteries of the Gospel: "angels long to look into these things" (1 Peter 1:12) (*All the Angels in the Bible*, p. 34, Herbert Lockyer).

4. We now go to Solomon's temple. Read 2 Chronicles 3:10-14. What was the wing span of one cherubim? _____

5. They (cherubs) are certainly not the nude valentine babies we see today with arrow in hand. Isn't it interesting what man can make of cherubim? By now you can tell that cherubim are angels that are very close to the throne of God and have a very intimate relationship with Him. Psalm 99:1, "The LORD... sits enthroned *between the cherubim.*" They never seem to carry a verbal message from God to men.

6. True or False: When we get to heaven, it will become obvious that God doesn't need the cherubim to add to His holiness, beauty and glory.

Seraphim

1. A Sunday School teacher asked her class to draw a picture from the Gospels. When she asked one boy what he was drawing he said, "God." She explained, "But no one has seen Him. We don't know what God looks like." To which the boy replied, "We will when I get done." Well, what that boy could't do the seraphim could do very easily. They are close to God, very, very close.

2. Seraphim literally means "burning ones," and they are inflamed in

their love for God. They are thought to be the highest rank of angels, and this is the only time they are mentioned in Scripture.

3. Read Isaiah 6:1-7. In spirit Isaiah is permitted to see the Lord, *Adonay*, the Ruler of all. What follows is an anthropomorphic description, that is, God and the throne room are described in human terms. How encompassing is the glory of God? _____

_____

4. Each seraphim had six wings. Two were used to cover their faces. Why? _____

Two wings were used to cover their feet. Why? _____

_____

Two wings were used to fly. For what purpose? _____

_____

In essence, four wings were employed for praise and two were used for service. Four for worship and two for work. We seem to reverse their priority. Should you think about spending more time in worship to the Lord and maybe a little less in work?

5. Who were the seraphim calling (crying) to? _____

They did this antiphonally which means _____

_____

To cry "holy" three times was in accordance with Hebrew idiom, and it recognized God as being extremely and perfectly holy.

6. In verse 3 the Lord is not called *Adonay* (v. 1) but *Yahweh Tzebaoth* or Lord of the covenant. Isaiah is permitted to hear the seraphim cry aloud their praise. How loud was the praise? _____

_____

7 What effect did all this have on Isaiah? _____

_____

How do you think this scene will impact on you in all reality when you step into the throne room of heaven? _____

_____

> The whole triumphant host give
> Thanks to God on high.
> "Hail, Father, Son, and Holy Ghost!"
> They ever cry.
> Hail, Ab'rams God and mine!
> I join the heav'nly lays:
> All might and majesty are Thine
> And endless praise.
>
> by Thomas Olivers

True or False: Once you are in the very presence of God in heaven you, too, will have a sense of your sinfulness.

True or False: It is difficult for God to let sin stay in His presence for very long.

8. The Lord recognizes Isaiah's confession by responding with a heavenly absolution. The Lord pardons and cleanses the sinner because of Calvary. Having received full forgiveness for all his sin,

   what is Isaiah compelled to do? _____

   _____

   And now, what about you? _____

   _____

Concluding Thoughts

We must make sure in this Bible study and in all things that our desire and interest in God is greater than that for angels. It is interesting that nowhere in Scripture are we commanded to pray to angels or to adore them. This is actually happening in our society today. We pray to God.

40

We adore God. We must be careful with this because man is so prone to put other things and persons in the place of God or before Him. And for the Scripture that we have studied in this Lesson we praise the Lord!

1. True or False: All holy angels are essentially the same.

2. True or False: In the Bible baby angels are called cherubs.

Closing Prayer

O Lord, Our Maker and Redeemer, we thank You for creating us and the angels. In a day when people want to treat angels like pets, You have told us much about them in this Lesson. What an army of heavenly hosts You have at Your disposal. What great desire they have to serve You in the area of responsibility You have assigned them. We stand amazed at the power and authority of Michael, and our hearts are warmed by the Gospel messages of Gabriel. The cherubim and seraphim must be very special to You. We earnestly anticipate the day when we will live with You and the blessed angels forever. Help us to especially see You, Lord Jesus, as our blessed Savior right now by faith. Help us to invite a friend to come to church with us next Sunday to meet You, Lord. We love You and want to honor You just as the angels do. In Your name we pray. Amen.

Closing Hymn

From all that dwell below the skies
Let the Creator's praise arise;
Alleluia, alleluia!
Let the Redeemer's name be sung
Through ev'ry land by ev'ry tongue.
Alleluia, alleluia, alleluia, alleluia, alleluia!

All praise to God the Father be,
All praise, eternal Son, to Thee;
Alleluia, alleluia!
Whom with the Spirit we adore
Forever and forevermore:
Alleluia, alleluia, alleluia, alleluia, alleluia!

41

Lesson 4

THE STORY OF ANGELS

The Angel of the Lord

Opening Hymn

All hail the pow'r of Jesus' name! Let angels prostrate fall;
Bring forth the royal diadem And crown Him Lord of all.
Bring forth the royal diadem And crown Him Lord of all.

O seed of Israel's chosen race, Now ransomed from the fall,
Hail Him who saves you by His grace And crown Him Lord of all.
Hail Him who saves you by His grace And crown Him Lord of all.

There are all kinds of angels, and — there is The Angel! "The angel of the Lord" (*malak Yahweh*). He appeared only in the Old Testament, never in the New Testament. He is a theophany, a manifestation of God before His incarnation. He is the preincarnate Son of God.

The Pharisees said to the Lord, "'You are not yet fifty years old and you have seen Abraham!' 'I tell you the truth,' Jesus answered, '*before Abraham was* born, I am!'" (John 8:57-58). On Maundy Thursday Jesus prayed, "And now, Father, glorify Me in Your presence with the glory I had with You *before the world began*" (John 17:5).

James Bjornstad correctly observes:

> To worship any other God whether angel, man or manmade image is idolatry. In Colossians 2 we are warned, "Let no one keep defrauding you of your prize by delighting in... the worship of angels" (Col. 2:18). We are not to worship angels and this is consistently demonstrated throughout the Bible. In

43

Revelation 19:19 an angel refuses worship from John. In Revelation 22:8-9, an angel refuses John's worship a second time, saying, "Do not do that... worship God." ...Yet Jesus is worshiped because He is God (*Understanding the Cults*, p. 45, by Josh McDowell and Don Stewart).

How does one know if an Old Testament verse is really referring to the preincarnate Christ? Here are some identifying marks.

... when He speaks not just for God but as God
... when He is described as only God can be described
... when He is worshiped as God alone should be worshiped
... when He does only what God could possibly do.

With these points as guidelines, let's examine a number of appearances of the Angel of the Lord in the Old Testament.

To Hagar

1. Read Genesis 16:1-10,13. This is the first appearance of the word "angel" in the Bible.

   What name is given this angel? _____

   _____ Notice the tender care of this Angel, the same care He had later when He came to earth in a body to seek and save the lost. Which verse shows how He made a promise that

   only God could make? _____ What does

   Hagar calls this Angel? _____

2. True or False: Hagar saw the Angel of the Lord with her own eyes, and she knew He was God. Defend your answer.

3. Read Genesis 21:14-19. What name is given this angel? _____

   _____

4. What does this section reveal about the preincarnate Son? _____

   _____

To Abraham and Sarah

Read Genesis 18:1-2,10,13. One of the three angels was really _____

What did the Lord promise them? _____

Tell how that affects you: _____

To Abraham and Isaac

Read Genesis 22:9-13,15-18. Abraham's faith had been severely tested earlier as he waited for a son, a son through whom the Savior of the world would come. Now another test. At the time of this text Isaac was 15 to 20 years old. He was as dear to his father as any child could be, but more so here because of the coming Messiah. God could not have given Abraham a more difficult test. "Abraham, I want your son, the one you've waited for for 100 years. I want you to give him to Me on an altar." As Abraham prepared to kill his son, he took a knife, raised it high above his head ready to plunge it into Isaac.

1. Who suddenly intervenes? _____

2. When the angel of the Lord speaks a second time He makes a promise that no created angel could make. What is it? _____

   _____

   _____

3. When we take an oath, who do we swear by and why? _____

   _____

4. Who does this angel swear by and why? _____

   _____

5. What do these verses reveal about the Lord? _____

   _____

To Jacob

1. Read Genesis 32:23-32. Jacob was a struggler. He struggled with Esau, then with Laban and now with God. He is all alone in the deep darkness of the night when suddenly another person struggles with him to throw him down. The struggle may have

45

lasted for several hours. Jacob's opponent does not speak a word. The wrestling stops the moment Jacob's hip is dislocated. The man cannot leave until Jacob permits it. By this time he knew whom he is wrestling with. This is a theophany, God appearing in human form. "*I will not let you go unless you bless me.*"

2. True or False: Jacob's wrestling is just as much spiritual as it is physical.

3 Why did Jacob call the name of this place Peniel? _____

_____

4. What does Hosea 12:3-5 tell us about the stranger? _____

_____

To Moses

1. Moses is now eighty years old and really, nothing great has been accomplished. For the last forty years he just herded sheep in the desert. But all that was about to change. Read Exodus 3:1-6,14-16. Who is this angel of the Lord, this *malach Yahveh?* He is the preincarnate Son of God! Verses 14-16 say that He is God!

True or False: It took Moses a while to figure out that the flame was supernatural.

The reaction of Moses is normal. He must look closer at this phenomenon.

2. "Here I am" indicated Moses' willingness to hear. God was in the burning bush. The ground was sacred. Moses' standing there barefoot was an expression of humility in the presence of divinity.

3. Reread the last sentence in verse 6. Why did Moses feel this way?

_____

The God of Abraham, Isaac and Jacob is the covenant God who promised the Seed, the Messiah. Just as the covenant God would forgive Abraham by his faith in the Messiah, we, too, are declared righteous by faith in the same Savior!

4. True or False: The Angel of the Lord, the preincarnate Son of God, calls Moses to lead His people out of Egypt to the Promised Land where He, the Messiah, will be born.

5. True or False: The Angel of the Lord almost always appears in the form of an angel.

To the Children of Israel

1. Read Exodus 13:21 and 14:19. Who was in the cloud and in the fire? _____

2. Read 1 Corinthians 10:1-4. Who was the rock? _____

   True or False: The Lord gave Israel both physical water and spiritual water.

3. True or False: Believers in the Old Testament and believers in the New Testament are really one people, one family because of their Savior.

To Manoah

1. Read Judges 13, the entire Chapter. Zorah was about 15 miles west of Jerusalem. The Angel of the Lord appeared to Manoah's barren wife with the promise of a son, Samson, who would be a Nazirite.

   How did Manoah's wife describe the Angel? _____

   _____

2. How did Manoah and his wife seem to act differently to the Angel of the Lord? _____

3. In verse 18 the Angel of the Lord says that His name is "beyond understanding." It could also be translated "wonderful." Think of Isaiah 9:6 when the Messiah is called "Wonderful Counselor." What amazing thing did the Angel of the Lord do during the sacrifice?

   _____

4. What is Manoah's final conclusion about this Angel? _____

_____

What is the thinking of his wife? _____

_____

To Joshua

1. Read Joshua 5:13-15. The "man" Joshua scouts the strongly fortified city of Jericho and meets someone who identifies himself as the "Commander of the army of the Lord." This would, of course,

   make Him _____

   Further, He reveals His divine character by _____

   from Joshua. With His sword drawn He indicates that He is ready to do battle for His nation, Israel. Think of it — He is the real Commander of Israel and the Commander of all the forces in heaven. Again, this makes Him the omnipotent Son of God. Here is the preincarnate Son issuing directives for entrance to the Promised Land so that

   something very, very important can take place there. What is it?

   _____

2. How is Joshua to show his reverence for this Commander? _____

   _____

   What does this suggest to us when we come before the Lord for

   worship? _____

3. What does the Commander in Chief, the Lord of lords and King of

   kings, do in 6:2-5? _____

   _____

To Gideon

1. Read Judges 6:11-24. The Lord calls Gideon a "mighty warrior" in verse 12. But how would you describe Gideon after rereading verses

   13, 15, and 17? _____

2. In what way did the Angel of the Lord encourage Gideon? _____

3. Someone has said, "Gideon intended a dinner. The Angel turned it into a sacrifice." Why do you suppose the Lord did this? _____

4. How would you describe the preincarnate Lord from these verses?

Concluding Thoughts

1. Isaac Watts wrote —

> Arrayed in mortal flesh,
> He like an Angel, stands,
> And holds the promises
> And pardons in His hands;
> Commissioned from His Father's throne,
> To make His grace to mortals known!
>
> Should all the hosts of death,
> And powers of hell unknown,
> Put their most dreadful forms
> Of rage and mischief on:
> I shall be safe! For Christ displays
> Superior power, and guardian grace!

2. The Angel of the Lord seems to appear at some critical point in the history of Israel or when His loving guidance or direction is needed by God's people. There are many more appearances of this special Angel beside the ones we have studied; there are even more appearances where we do not know for sure whether it is this Angel or some other angel. His Old Testament appearances seem to prefigure His New Testament ministry.

3. Appearances of the Angel of the Lord stopped after Jesus' incarnation. Why do you suppose this happened? _____

_____

4. How did the Old Testament believers demonstrate that they recognized who the Angel of the Lord really was? _____

_____

Closing Prayer

Dear Lord Jesus, a thousand thanks to You for revealing Yourself so often to Your children in the Old Testament. You spoke not just for God but as God. You were worshiped as God alone should be worshiped. And You did what only God could possibly do. Show Your tender mercies to us as You did to Hagar. May we wrestle with You in prayer for Your daily blessing. As You victoriously led Israel to the Promised Land, so lead us day by day on our journey to the new Jerusalem. May we listen to Your instructions to us through daily Bible study even as Joshua and Gideon listened to Your instructions and won great battles against the forces of evil. Lead us on, O King Eternal, until we cross the Jordan and join all the saints and angelic hosts to serve and praise You, world without end! In Your name. Amen.

Closing Hymn

Hail Him, you heirs of David's line,
Whom David Lord did call,
The God Incarnate, man divine,
And crown Him Lord of all.
The God Incarnate, man divine,
And crown Him Lord of all.

Oh, that with yonder sacred throng
We at His feet may fall!
We'll join the everlasting song
And crown Him Lord of all.
We'll join the everlasting song
And crown Him Lord of all.

THE STORY OF ANGELS

Guarding and Avenging Angels

Opening Hymn

Holy God, we praise Your name;
Lord of all, we bow before You.
All on earth Your scepter claim,
All in heav'n above adore You.
Infinite Your vast domain,
Everlasting is Your reign.

Hark! The glad celestial hymn
Angel choirs above are raising;
Cherubim and seraphim,
In unceasing chorus praising,
Fill the heav'ns with sweet accord:
"Holy, holy, holy Lord!"

What do angels do for work? There are a lot of ideas around, many of which are totally unScriptural. For example —

Angels have fun ways of letting us know they are around. They arrange coincidences and favorable meetings to get our attention. They also let us know they're with us by providing humor (attacks of hilarity and mirth) during serious events; giving us unexplainable feelings of peace and well-being during trying times; surround us with "good luck" and fortunate situations; leaving an exquisite scent in the air resembling roses or jasmine, which may intoxicate our minds for a moment; helping feelings of true hope and optimism glow in our hearts; and providing peak experiences of joy and love that sometimes rush through us (*Guardians of Hope*, p. 21, by Terry Lynn Taylor).

On the other hand there are Christians who can attest to the activity of angels in their personal lives.

As an evangelist I have often felt too far spent to minister from the pulpit to men and women who have filled stadiums to hear a message from the Lord. Yet again and again my weariness has vanished, and my strength has been renewed. I have been filled with God's power not only in my soul but physically. On many occasions God has become especially real, and has sent His unseen angelic visitors to touch my body to let me be His messenger for heaven, speaking as a dying man to dying men. We may not always be aware of the presence of angels. We can't always predict how they will appear. But angels have been said to be our neighbors. Often they may be our companions without our being aware of their presence. We know little of their constant ministry. The Bible assures us, however, that one day our eyes will be unscaled to see and know the full extent of the attention angels have given us (1 Corinthians 13:11-12) (*Angels: God's Secret Agents*, pp. 73,74, by Billy Graham).

Guarding Angels

Corrie ten Boom is now in heaven with her Lord, but before she left earth she experienced many heavy trials. We look at just one.

Why did the Lord ask anything so hard from us? I pleaded, "O Lord, if Thou dost nevertheless ask this sacrifice of us, give us the strength to offer it; give us the willingness to make it..."

For a few minutes we were quiet and spoke softly with the Saviour. He was with us and knew what we were suffering, and He loved us. "Corrie, I am ready," whispered Betsie softly. "Then everything is all right," I answered.

I took her arm, and together we entered the terrifying building. At a table were women who took away all our possessions. Everyone had to undress completely and then go to a room where her hair was checked.

I asked a woman who was busy checking the possessions of the new arrivals if I might use the toilet. She pointed to a door, and I discovered that convenience was nothing more than a hole in the shower-room floor. Betsie stayed close beside me all the time. Suddenly I had an inspiration. "Quick, take off your woollen underwear," I whispered to her. I rolled it up with mine and laid the bundle in a corner with my little Bible. The spot was alive with cockroaches, but I didn't worry about that. I felt wonderfully relieved and happy. "The Lord is busy answering our prayers, Betsie," I whispered, "we shall not have to make the sacrifice of all our clothes."

We hurried back to the row of women waiting to be undressed. A little later, after we had our showers and put on our shirts and shabby dresses, I hid the roll of underwear and my Bible under my dress. It did bulge out obviously through my dress; but I prayed, "Lord, cause now Thine angels to surround me; and let them not be transparent today, for the guards must not see me." I felt perfectly at ease. Calmly I passed the guards. Everyone was checked, from the front, the sides, the back. Not a bulge escaped the eyes of the guard. The woman just in front of me had hidden a woollen vest under her dress; it was taken from her. They let me pass, for they did not see me. Betsie, right behind me, was searched.

But outside awaited another danger. On each side of the door were women who looked everyone over for the second time. They felt over the body of each one who passed. I knew that they would not see me, for the angels were still surrounding me. I was not even surprised when they passed me by; but within me rose the jubilant cry, "O Lord, if Thou dost so answer prayer, I can face even Ravensbruck unafraid" (*A Prisoner and yet...*, pp. 82-83, Corrie ten Boom).

Yes, some angels guard, and they guard well! Let's take a look.

- **AT THE GARDEN OF EDEN**

1. Read Genesis 3:24. How would you describe the work of the Cherubim here? _____

2. What are they guarding? _____

3. Why do you think Adam and Eve did not even try to go back into the Garden? _____

4. Any message for us here? _____

- **WITH ELIJAH**

Read 1 Kings 19:1-9. Elijah was filled with despair and asked the Lord to take his life. What did the angel do? _____

_____

- **WITH ELISHA**

1. Read 2 Kings 6:13-17. What did Elisha's servant see first? _____

_____

2. What did the servant see just a little later? _____

_____

3. How was this possible? _____

4. What do you think you would see if the Lord "opened your eyes" in similar fashion? _____

5. How does that make you feel? _____

Thus the prophet's servant saw, When the Syrian host assailed,
Every heavenly warrior And bright encampment all unveiled.

And from yonder distant sky, All conflict we shall view:
Turn and see the dangers fly, And praise God that led us through.

(Edmeston)

- **WITH DAVID**

1. Read Psalm 91:9-12. This is a Psalm of David. Here is a marvelous promise by God to every believer. How will God go about executing

Dr. James Dobson tells of a mother who sent him a letter about her four year old daughter. The daughter had just started attending Sunday School. The little girl proudly announced to her mother that she would no longer be afraid of the dark. When the mother asked "Why?", the girl said that she had just learned in Sunday School that she had a "gargling" angel to protect her.

His care for His own according to these verses?

_____

2. What two things will the angels do? _____

_____

_____

_____

3. True or False: These words do not prove that every believer has a guardian angel at all times, but they do prove that God will use them for that purpose when and where He sees fit.

- **WITH SHADRACH, MESHACH AND ABEDNEGO**

1. Read Daniel 3:24-28. Daniel's three companions faced a terrible death. Two things amazed the King as he looked. What were they?

_____

2. The fourth person was either the Son of God or an angel. Either way, what was the net result for the three young men? _____

_____

- **WITH DANIEL**

1. Read Daniel 6:18-23. How did God choose to go about saving Daniel's life? _____

2. True or False: God could have saved David's life by direct intervention.

3. True or False: It must please God to occasionally demonstrate His care for His children through the work of a visible angel.

- **WITH THE APOSTLES**

55

1. Read Acts 5:17-20. "More and more men and women believed in the Lord and were added to their number" (v. 14). The Sadducees were filled with jealousy and anger and so all of the Apostles were arrested by the Temple police. In one swift stroke the leaders of the church were removed. The Devil knows how to work, doesn't he? But the Lord is wiser and stronger than Satan. During the night an angel appears, miraculously opens the locked doors, and leads the Apostles out. Why do you suppose the guards did not stop the angel? _____

2. What does the angel instruct the Apostles to do? _____

    _____

3. Where do you think this angel is getting all of his orders from?

    _____

*   **WITH PETER**

1. Read Acts 12:1-17. Peter was to be executed as a favor to the Jews who opposed the Gospel. What were Peter's chances of escaping from this imprisonment? _____

2. What happened to Peter's chains? _____

    To the prison door? _____

3. Peter went to the house of Mary where many believers were praying for Peter's release. How did Rhoda react to Peter's appearance at the door? _____

    How did the believers react to Rhoda's announcement? _____

    _____

    True or False: The believers should not have been surprised that Peter was at the door. Defend your answer.

4. What do you learn about guarding angels from this episode? ____

    _____

5. In one sentence, how do you think Peter's testimony on angels

56

would go? _____

_____

- ## WITH PAUL

1. Read Acts 27:19-25. The crew were pagans. Paul had to reach Rome in safety so that he could give a witness to Caesar. But first Paul gave a witness to the crew concerning His God and the protection that was promised.

    True or False: God saved the crew because of the presence of and for the sake of the safety of Paul.

    What does this say about the benefit of a Christian in the presence

    of unbelievers? _____

    Do you suppose the crew believed Paul or laughed at him? _____

2. True or False: Whenever one of God's children is in danger, God will send an angel to deliver him.

    > In the last chapter of this book we see the great apostle Paul in a Roman prison. No angel appeared to open his prison door. And when later he is condemned to die, no angel comes to arrest the arm of the executioner. Throughout this age thousands upon thousands, tens of thousands, yea hundreds of thousands of Christians were cast into vile prisons, cruelly tortured and finally put to death in a merciless manner. No angels came to deliver them. The heavens are silent (*The Angels of God*, p. 90, by A. C. Gaebelein).

    Why does this happen? Why does God not always intervene directly

    when we are in danger or indirectly through angels? _____

    _____

3.   Ellen Olender, Florida — I was at a metaphysical healing circle when the leader told us this story: An elderly lady I know took her cat to the vet. Unfortunately, the cat needed to be put to sleep. The lady sat in the waiting room and looked out the window. She saw her cat in the arms of an angel. The angel had the face of a cat and looked at the cat with sheer love and care. Cradling the cat gently, the angel ascended. Every time I

tell this story, I get chills of affirmation" (*Answers From the Angels*, p. 145, by Terry Lynn Taylor and Friends).

If you do not get chills of affirmation when reading this account, what do you get? _____

_____

Avenging Angels

Angels have many tasks to perform.

The Bible says that throughout history angels have worked to carry out God's judgments, directing the destinies of nations disobedient to God. For example, God used angels in scattering the people of Israel because of their sins" (*Angels: God's Secret Agents*, p. 99, by Billy Graham).

In Hebrews 1:7 we read, "He makes His angels winds, His servants *flames of fire.*" Another example, "Do not grumble, as some of them did — and were killed by the *destroying angel*" (1 Corinthians 10:10). Let's take a closer look at avenging angels.

• SODOM AND GOMORRAH

1. Read Genesis 19:1-13. In what two ways did these angels demonstrate that they were avenging angels? _____

_____

2. True or False: The Lord directly commissioned these angels to be agents of destruction.

• PLAGUES IN EGYPT

1. Read Exodus 12:12-13. What was the Lord going to do? _____

_____

2. Read Psalm 78:49-51. What are the Lord's agents called? _____

58

- **185,000 Assyrians**

1. Read 2 Kings 19:20,22,35. Here is the response by God to Hezekiah's prayer. The Assyrian soldiers were well known for their battle skills. It was the night before the attack on Jerusalem. How many angels did God use to totally crush the Assyrian army? ___

2. More soldiers were killed in this one night than those killed in the atomic blasts at Hiroshima and Nagasaki. Jesus said, "Do you think I cannot call on My Father, and He will at once put at My disposal more than twelve legions of angels?" (Matthew 26:53). If only one angel could annihilate the Assyrian army in one night, what do you think 72,000 of them could do? _____

- **Herod**

1. Read Acts 12:21-23. Herod was celebrating a festival in honor of Claudius Caesar and was wearing his royal robes. The historian Josephus describes the festal robe as a dazzling, bright silver robe. What did the people, most of whom were pagan, say when Herod spoke? _____

2. God says, "I am the LORD; that is My name! I will not give My glory to another or My praise to idols" (Isaiah 42:8). Herod was a Jew. When the people proclaimed that he was a god, he did not deny it. He permitted the blasphemy. What did the Lord do? _____

    _____

    How would you describe the way in which Herod died? _____

    _____

3. Apparently the angel was not seen by anyone. Herod, who persecuted the Christians, came to a painful end. What does verse 24 tell us? _____

Concluding Thoughts

59

We have briefly looked at a Biblical history of guarding and avenging angels. We have this instance of God withdrawing an avenging angel: "So the LORD sent a plague on Israel, and seventy thousand men of Israel fell dead. And God sent an angel to destroy Jerusalem. But as the angel was doing so, the LORD saw it and was grieved because of the calamity and said to the angel who was destroying the people, 'Enough! Withdraw your hand.' The angel of the LORD was then standing at the threshing floor of Araunah the Jebusite. David looked up and saw the angel of the LORD standing between heaven and earth, with a drawn sword in his hand extended over Jerusalem. Then David and the elders, clothed in sackcloth, fell face down" (1 Chronicles 21:14-16).

True or False: None of the believers mentioned in this Lesson asked the angels for information or for anything. This stands in direct contrast to some people today who tell us to ask for information, protection, etc., from guardian angels. If you marked this true, what is their "problem"? _____

Closing Prayer

We rejoice, O Lord, at Your words which describe the activity of the angels. We see the awesome power You have given angels as they served as agents of death and destruction in Bible times. You posted them as guards at the Garden of Eden. You sent them to serve Elijah, Elisha, David, the Apostles, Peter, Paul, and many, many other saints. When it is necessary, O Lord, and in Your wisdom, may Your angels guard and keep us throughout life and in the hour of death. O Lord, forgive us our sins for the sake of Your suffering and death upon the cross. Continue to instruct us in this Bible study. Give us grace to serve You faithfully even as the angels serve You. We pray in Your name. Amen.

Closing Hymn

You are King of Glory, Christ; Son of God, yet born of Mary.
For us sinners sacrificed, As to death a Tributary,
First to break the bars of death, You have opened heav'n to faith.

Holy Father, Holy Son, Holy Spirit, three we name You,
Though in essence only one; Undivided God we claim You
And, adoring, bend the knee While we own the mystery.

THE STORY OF ANGELS

Watching and Communicating Angels

Opening Hymn

Immortal, invisible, God only wise,
In light inaccessible hid from our eyes,
Most blessed, most glorious, O Ancient of Days,
Almighty, victorious, Your great name we praise!

Unresting, unhasting, and silent as light,
Nor wanting nor wasting, You rule in Your might;
Your justice like mountains high soaring above,
Your clouds which are fountains of goodness and love.

We have learned a great deal about angels so far in Holy Scripture. What else do the holy angels do? Perhaps it would be good to note what they don't do. Example:

Angels are always available to help you create heaven in your life. There are angels for every occasion, including angels, such as guardians, spiritual guides, cheerleaders, and soul angels, who are always with us; angels of the moment, such as healers, miracle engineers and rescuers; angels who embellish human life, such as worry extinguishers, fun executives, and prosperity brokers; nature devas, who watch over and help Mother Nature; and even designer angels, who can help with almost any task you assign. Angels' primary concern is to help transform human attitudes toward the positive, lighter side of life" (*Guardians of Hope*, p. 38, by Terry Lynn Taylor).

Remember, there are many people who really believe this and the following.

> Keri was a frequent student at our classes. She came to class nearly every week but never heard really well. Finally, she came to us and asked if she was doing something wrong. We assured her she wasn't and we decided to talk to her angel for her to find out why she was not connecting. We could not hear her angel either! Only about every third word made sense. In frustration, we said, "Come on, angels, we need someone louder. Send an angel with a bigger voice!" A booming-voiced angel came in with a wonderful, clear, exciting, and comforting message. What was wrong? Nothing. The angel with whom Keri had connected was a very tiny angel named Amelia. She was dainty and feminine and had a little voice to go with her diminutive body. When we found out what Amelia's work was, everyone understood why her voice was difficult to hear. Amelia's primary job in the universe is to whisper into ears of babies how much God loves them (*Angelspeake*, p. 74, by Barbara Mark & Trudy Griswold).

Kind of cute, isn't it? But totally nonScriptural, totally! What does the Bible say? We continue our study. *The Story of Angels — Watching and Communicating Angels!*

Let's turn to Scripture. Read Zechariah 1:8-10.

In a miraculous way the Lord gave Zechariah the vision. The Angel of the Lord (v. 11) is the Commander of all angels, Jesus. He sent His holy angels to observe various countries. Clearly they had been sent to watch and report. In this Lesson we will focus on the watching and communicating of the holy angels. Be appraised that while they deliver messages to the Lord and from the Lord, they never deliver messages from us to the Lord.

Deliver the Law

Acts 7:53 — "You who have received the law that was put into effect *through angels* but have not obeyed it." Angels were active in the giving of the Law on Mount Sinai. They were associated in its transference by

God to Moses.

Galatians 3:19b — "The law was put into effect *through angels* by a Mediator." The Mediator is Christ. We do not know exactly what the angels did in giving the Law to Moses. Jews were proud of the Law. They regarded the Law as ordained by angels, but they failed to keep the Law, and they failed to recognize the Mediator who gave it, the Lord Jesus.

Hebrews 2:2-3 — "For if the message spoken *by angels* was binding, and every violation and disobedience received its just punishment, how shall we escape if we ignore such a great salvation?" The "message" was the Law which God gave on Sinai. The angels participated in the giving of the Law in some way, but we do not have the details.

True or False: In all three Scriptures it becomes apparent that God thought it very important to employ the services of holy angels in the presentation of the Law to men.

Balaam and His Donkey

1. To introduce you to Balaam's mentality I share these two quotes from a newspaper:

   I live in a semi-rural area. We recently had a new neighbor call the local township administrative office to request the removal of the Deer Crossing sign on our road. The reason: Many deer were being hit by cars and he no longer wanted them to cross there.

   My daughter went to the local Taco Bell and ordered a taco. She asked the individual behind the counter for "minimal lettuce." He said he was sorry, but they only had iceberg.

   Now these people are dense. This is Balaam! Read Numbers 22:21-35.

2. Balaam was a celebrity, an internationally known seer — a magician and prophet. He could see what other people couldn't see. King Balak hired him to curse Israel.

God was angry with Balaam and his wicked plans. How did God decide to stop Balaam? _____

What kind of angel was this? _____

The donkey could see the angel, but Balaam couldn't, so he beat his donkey with his staff. Who is the real "jackass" in this story?

_____ Balaam says that if he had a sword he

would _____ the donkey. The Lord opened his eyes and

Balaam saw the angel standing in the road with a _____

_____ As we further study Balaam, we notice that he learned nothing from this incident. He refused to let God keep him from sin.

3. What lesson is there for you from this story? _____

_____

_____

Daniel

Daniel 4:13 reads, "In the visions I saw while lying in my bed, I looked, and there before me was a *messenger*, a *holy one*, coming down from heaven." Daniel 4:17, "The decision is announced by *messengers*, the *holy ones* declare the verdict, so that the living may know that the Most High is sovereign over the kingdoms of men..." Daniel 4:23, "You, O king, saw a *messenger*, a *holy one*, coming down from heaven and saying, 'Cut down the tree and destroy it, but leave the stump, bound with iron and bronze, in the grass of the field, while its roots remain in the ground....'"

We might call these angels messengers — watchmen! Angels watch. They do not slumber nor sleep, but they are in constant service to their great God, and they are holy, absolutely pure.

Mary and Joseph

1. Luke 1:35, "The *angel* answered, 'The Holy Spirit will come upon you, and the power of the Most High will overshadow you. So the Holy One to be born will be called the Son of God.'"

64

Matthew 1:20, "An *angel* of the Lord appeared to him in a dream and said, 'Joseph son of David, do not be afraid to take Mary home as your wife, because what is conceived in her is from the Holy Spirit.'"

Matthew 2:13, "When they had gone, an *angel* of the Lord appeared to Joseph in a dream. 'Get up,' he said, 'take the Child and His mother and escape to Egypt. Stay there until I tell you, for Herod is going to search for the child to kill Him.'"

2. What is the role and function of angels in these verses? _____

Spectators of Apostles' Martyrdom

1. Read 1 Corinthians 4:9. Rome made a public exhibition of the many executions that took place in their amphitheaters. That is what happened to the apostles as they were put to death. They were put on display just like the Lord. They were on display not just to the world, but to the whole universe. Paul says there is a cosmic dimension to the exhibition — seen not only by men but also by the holy angels

2. Why might the angels have seen much more of the apostles' suffering and dying than men? _____

_____

3. What thoughts do you suppose went through the minds of the angels as they viewed the violent deaths which all the apostles, except John, went through? _____

_____

4. In what way might the angels envy the apostles? _____

_____

Peer into Salvation

1. A hopeless romantic sprayed this message on an overpass on a busy freeway in Kansas City: "JEFFREY & PATTI = LOVE FOREVER AND EVER 125% TRUE." One is a little suspicious of just how true their love is at 125%. **God's love for sinful mankind is 100% true!** The Bible guarantees it. That really intrigues the angels! Read 1 Peter 1:10-12 with special emphasis on the last sentence.

2. The angels watched God as He fashioned man's body out of the dust of the ground and, breathing into him, communicated to this creature immortality. What shouts of joy must have come from them when man, the crown of all the earth, stood before his Creator, made a little lower than themselves, the angels... With what horror, then, they must have watched when the serpent, Satan, whom they knew so well, sneaked up to the woman and the fatal conversation began. If angels can weep and demons laugh... angels must have wept in deepest agony, while the demon-world shouted for joy.

   And now the history of redemption begins. There is to be enmity between the serpent and the woman, between the seed of the woman and the seed of the serpent. There is to appear the seed of the woman to crush the serpent's head... Now, angels begin in their eager desire to look into these things, the things concerning Him who is to come, concerning His suffering... He comes to take on the body of the first man and that body is called into existence by a creative act of the third person of the Holy Trinity. He Himself, the Highest, is going to overshadow the Virgin, to unite Himself with that body. Here is the great mystery over which the innumerable hosts of angels pondered in holy awe (*The Angels of God*, pp. 54-55,64, by A. C. Gaebelein).

3. "Even angels long to *look into* these things." The Greek "to look into" does not mean to glance at, but to stoop and look intently, to look to understand. It also conveys the thought that when the angels do this, they still cannot fully grasp the Gospel message as it applies to Christ and then to us. One reason why the angels have difficulty fully understanding might be _____

   _____

4. Why do you suppose they try diligently to understand the Gospel

mystery? _____

_____

Worship

1. Read 1 Corinthians 11:10. A man's head is to be bare (v. 7), but a woman's covered in that day. Paul is not laying down a law that is to apply for all time. In that day she "ought" to worship with a covered head. But she is also to do so "because of the angels."

   True or False: Paul was fairly convinced that angels observe believers when they worship.

2. Why do you suppose angels are intrigued by the worship of believers? _____

_____

_____

3. True or False: It would appear that God wants the angels to see the results of His love for men expressed by them when they worship Him.

4. Give several reasons why you should pay attention to your worship activity and habits: _____

_____

_____

Philip

1. Read Acts 8:26-29. The Ethiopian nobleman, a black man, a man of power and authority would become the first Gentile convert. He was not a pagan, but a proselyte (A Gentile committed to observing the law who lived among the Jews, but still regarded as a Gentile by all Jews). Who did the Lord employ to bring the evangelist and the first Gentile convert together? _____

67

The _____ informs Philip which _____ to take. The _____ knew that the Ethiopian was reading _____ The _____ could not preach the Gospel, but _____ could. Why didn't God just send the angel to instruct and baptize the Ethiopian? _____

2. How do you think the truths of this Scripture play out today and what are their implications(Be specific)? _____

_____

_____

Cornelius

1. Read Acts 10:1-8. Caesarea was 30 miles north of Joppa. There Cornelius served as a Roman army officer in charge of 100 men. How did he impact on others? _____

_____

They were proselytes of the gate, Gentiles who were prevented from going beyond the court of the Gentiles in the Temple. Cornelius developed the two great virtues of the Jewish faith, namely: _____

_____

Suddenly he distinctly sees and hears an angel. What is his first reaction? _____ He addresses the angel as "Lord," meaning that he regarded the angel as superior. The good works of Cornelius are accepted as good works flowing out of a heart filled with faith. God was going to use Cornelius for a great purpose, so that the Gospel would be preached to all Gentiles.

2. Describe the function and purpose of this angel? _____

_____

_____

John's Revelation

1. For every revelation it is imperative to know the source. Robert Burns wrote of John —

    How he, who lone on Patmos banished,
    Saw in the sun a mighty angel stand;
    And heard great Babylon's doom pronounc'd by
    Heaven's command.

In chains John is sent to the island of Patmos. Here he receives an awesome revelation — hence the name of this last Book of Scripture. It is unique for many reasons among which is this — Revelation is the ANGEL BOOK in the New Testament. Angels are found everywhere.

2. Read Revelation 1:1-2 and 22:6. Precisely what does the Lord do through an angel? _____

    _____

    _____

Suggestion: Read the Book of Revelation at home during the next seven days (three chapters a day).

Concluding Thoughts

Not only does God watch us and know us day by day, sometimes the angels do, too. They are spectators to the plan of salvation. They peer into the mysteries of salvation with inquisitive minds endeavoring to understand. And they are communicators, bringing messages from the Lord to His children on earth. Billy Graham describes one important facet of this.

While God has delegated angels to make special pronouncements for Him, He has not given them the privilege of proclaiming the Gospel message... notice what the writer says:

Holy, Holy is what the angels sing,
And I expect to help them make the courts of heaven ring.

69

And when I sing redemption's story,
They will fold their wings,
For angels never felt the joy that our salvation brings.

No angel can be an evangelist. No angel can pastor a church, although angels watch over particular churches. No angel can do counseling. No angel can enjoy sonship in Jesus or be a partaker of the divine nature or become a joint heir with Jesus in His kingdom. You and I are a unique and royal priesthood in the universe, and we have privileges that even angels cannot experience (*Angels: God's Secret Agents*, pp. 111-113).

Closing Prayer

Holy and righteous God, how can we ever thank You for all Your mercies extended toward us? We are sorry that so many people have so many far-out ideas about the angels. We are very grateful for what You tell us about them. May we not be like Balaam who wouldn't listen to You. May we eagerly look into everything You teach us in the Bible. While angels cannot understand salvation, we can at least believe it and praise You for it. Enlighten our minds and hearts that we never take our redemption on the Cross for granted. O God, we praise You and worship You for the gift of Jesus! Holy Spirit, please come and richly bless our corporate and individual worship — not just because angels may be watching, but because You are watching. Thank You for all the Bible saints. Thank You for all the angels. Thank You for the Revelation given to John. With joy and great anticipation we look forward to joining the redeemed and the holy angels in praising and serving You forever and ever. In the name of Jesus! Amen.

Closing Hymn

All life You engender in great and in small;
To all life befriender, the true life of all.
We blossom and flourish in richness and range,
We wither and perish, but You never change.

Great Father of glory, pure Father of light,
Your angels adore You, enveiling their sight.
All laud we would render, oh, lead us to see
The light of Your splendor, Your love's majesty!

Lesson 7

THE STORY OF ANGELS

Angels and Jesus

Opening Hymn

Hark! the herald angels sing, "Glory to the newborn King:
Peace on earth, and mercy mild, God and sinners reconciled!"
Joyful, all ye nations, rise, Join the triumph of the skies;
With the angelic host proclaim, "Christ is born in Bethlehem!"
Hark! the herald angels sing, "Glory to the newborn King."

Hail the heaven-born Prince of Peace, Hail the Sun of Righteousness!
Light and life to all He brings, Risen with healing in His wings.
Mild He lays His glory by, Born that man no more may die;
Born to raise the sons of earth, Born to give them second birth.
Hark! the herald angels sing, "Glory to the newborn King."

My wife received a Hallmark Card on angels from five non-Christian friends. It reads:

> The angel in your life may smile on you today when you look into the blossom of a flower. The angel in your life may blow a gentle kiss your way that fills your soul with strong creative power. The angel in your life may sprinkle sunshine on your path to let you know you're where you need to be. And if you pay attention to the angel in your life, you'll feel a sense of sweet serenity.

Gushy — eh? But by now we know that according to the Bible the form and function of angels is quit different from what man thinks. The story of angels continues in this Lesson — angels and Jesus! Just think of it — the Lord created them in the beginning. They worshiped Him

71

in heaven and carried out His orders here on earth throughout the Old Testament era. And they were commanded to continue to worship and obey Him while He was the God-Man here on earth.

> Beyond all question, the mystery of godliness is great: He (Jesus) appeared in a body, was vindicated by the Spirit, was *seen by angels*, was preached among the nations, was believed on in the world, was taken up in glory (1 Timothy 3:16).

And again, when God brings His firstborn into the world, He says, "Let all God's *angels* worship Him" (Hebrews 1:6).

We will study the major events in our Lord's earthly life when angels played a key function.

Before His Birth

● WITH ZECHARIAH AND ELIZABETH

1. Many years ago the hymn writer Joseph Griff wrote this amazing verse:

> Jesus! Oh, how can it be true,
> A mortal man ashamed of You?
> Ashamed of You, whom angels praise,
> Whose glories shine through endless days?

Christian friend, never, never be ashamed of Jesus. Angels are not ashamed of Him, but an important Bible character came close to doing just that. Four hundred years of silence was now to coming to an end. God was getting ready to send His Son. Read Luke 1:5-22.

2. What was Zechariah's first reaction to seeing the holy angel?

_____ Zechariah had stopped praying for a child because of age.

True or False: Zechariah believed the message of the angel, but he did seem to have some doubt. Defend your answer.

The angel describes John's great work as the forerunner of the Messiah. But Zechariah continues to doubt.

True or False: When Abraham was told that he would have a

72

son(Isaac) in old age, he questioned but believed, whereas, Zechariah questioned and did not believe.

If you were Zechariah, would you have believed? Either way, why?

_____

Gabriel means "man of God." He stands in the very presence of God. Which words of Gabriel strongly suggest that Zechariah better start believing the message? _____

_____

3. What do you learn about Gabriel from this incident? _____

_____

_____

● WITH MARY AND JOSEPH

1. Read Luke 1:26-28,30-31. The angel's name

   was _____, and he was sent by

   _____ How is Mary's reaction

   different from Zechariah's? _____

   _____ Gabriel answers

   each _____ that Mary puts to him.

2. Read Matthew 1:20-24. We assume that this angel is the _____ angel that appeared to Mary. He came to Joseph in a _____ This was not a silly dream like ours might be. Joseph actually saw and heard the _____ What does the angel say the mission of this Child will be? _____

   What was Joseph's response? _____

3. What do these two incidents tell us about angels? _____

   _____

4. What feelings do you think the angelic hosts must have had when

they watched the Son of God, their Creator, become a little Baby in Mary? _____

5. Here is an interesting thought:

    He Himself, the Highest, is going to overshadow the Virgin, to unite Himself with that body. Here is the great mystery over which the innumerably hosts of angels pondered in holy awe. What must be their feeling when they see man, the creature of the dust, for whom God sent His only Son... refusing to believe in Him whom the Father sent (*The Angels of God*, p. 64, by A. C. Gabelein)?

    What do you think the answer is to the above question? _____

    _____

At His Birth

1. Read Luke 2:8-15. The greatest night in world history has now come. All of heaven is astir because of what is happening. All the angelic host are fully aware and excited. The earth alone is ignorant of what has just happened. In an instant a holy angel appears to the shepherds, and the light of his glory floods the sky and the fields. The awe-inspiring angel fills their hearts with fear and sends a chill down

    their backs, and his first words are: _____

    _____ The shepherds were among the faithful in Israel waiting for the promised Redeemer King. But it's the message, not the messenger that is all-important! To them and all mankind a Savior is born; not a Savior from cancer or war or old age, but from sin and death and hell! And He is for everyone!

2. When the angel has finished announcing the Good News, God fills the sky with _____ In Greek they are called a πληθοσ, which is a "great number." The host which fills the sky is a part of the great heavenly army. Together they give glory to God "in the

highest" for sending His Son to redeem the fallen human race.
Why should they care this much? _____

_____

Sulking most of all, we can be sure, was the instigator of all idolatry: Satan. As the holy angels sang an anthem to the glory of God, the evil ones kept a sullen silence. Celebrate because the Savior was born? Never! (*With Jesus Every Day*, p. 358, Rudolph F. Norden).

How does the above comment make you feel? _____

_____

True or False: The sky above the shepherds could not have held all the hosts of heaven.

The angels in the sky did not disappear, but _____

For His Safety

1. God recognizes Joseph as the foster-father of Jesus. Read Matthew 2:13-14,19-20.

2. Why do you suppose Joseph did not take any time to think over the message of the angel? _____

_____

3 True or False: God communicates rather directly with Joseph through the angel.

4 How long was Joseph to remain in Egypt? _____

_____

5. True or False: It would be fair to assume that there were many angels who kept watch over the Child while He was in Egypt.

The Temptation

1. Read Matthew 4:10-11. The Devil left, and the angels came. They did not come during the temptation, but after. The word

75

"attended" (διηκονουν) carries the idea of ministering and the spreading of a table for nourishment and strength. Think of the story of Elijah. An angel came to him and provided bread and water (1 Kings 19:5-8).

2. How does this ministry play a key part in the plan of salvation?

_____

3. What truth is the Lord emphasizing in Matthew 26:53? _____

_____

_____

In Gethsemane

1. Read Luke 22:42-44. Peter, James, and John were brought along to encourage the Lord, but instead they _____

2. What did Jesus ask His Father? _____

_____

What was the Father's answer? _____

_____

3. What does verse 44 suggest? _____

_____

What might have happened if the Lord had not been strengthened by the angel?

_____

_____

The Son of God in tears,
Angels with wonder see;
Be thou astonished, O my soul,
He shed those tears for thee!

Author Unknown

At His Resurrection

1. When Jesus hung on the cross, suffering the punishment for all sinners of all time, no angel came to comfort and strengthen Him. He was alone, all alone, forsaken even by His heavenly Father. Then He died and was buried. Everything is about to change. Read Matthew 28:2-7.

2. No angel is needed to open the tomb so that the Lord can appear. He is already risen from the dead. An angel came to the site, and there is an earthquake. Two engineering professors at Georgia Tech say that a stone of the kind used to close sepulchers in the these times would have weighed a minimum of 1.5 to 2 tons.

> Angels roll the rock away:
> Death yields up his mighty prey.
> Jesus, rising from the tomb,
> Scatters all its fearful gloom!
>
> by Dr. Gibbons

The angel removes the stone from the entrance with little effort and then _____ on it. The angel looks like _____ and his clothes are like _____ The soldiers are so shocked at the sight that they look like _____ What do you suppose you will feel like when you see ALL the heavenly host in the new Jerusalem? _____ _____ We cannot think of anything in this world as bright and pure as these holy angels. But something else will really catch your eye then. What will it be? _____

2. John tells us that there were two angels in the tomb. But the one on the outside, sitting on the stone, had the message that both we and the women need desperately to hear: "He is risen — just as He said." Then they are told to bring this Good News to the disciples.

3. On a scale of 1 to 10, how high do you think the women would rate the sight and message of the angel that Easter Sunday? _____

At His Ascension

1. Read Acts 1:9-11. The Lord has finished speaking. Everyone's eyes are focused on Him. Luke tells us that as He blessed them He rose into the sky. Majestically and mightily He rises higher and higher. The disciples eyes are wide open in astonishment. They continue to stare, hoping for one last look at their dear Lord. Suddenly He is gone. He has ascended into heaven. What happened as they looked into the sky? _____

_____

They appeared as _____ dressed in _____

Frequently the angels appear as young men, pictures of strength and beauty, but they never appear as women. The white apparel signifies purity and holiness.

2. What message do the angels give the disciples? _____
_____

3. How would you describe the purpose of the angels? _____
_____
_____

Concluding Thoughts

1. St. Paul writes in 1 Timothy 3:16, "Beyond all question, the mystery of godliness is great: He (Jesus) appeared in a body, was vindicated by the Spirit, was *seen by angels*, was preached among the nations, was believed on in the world, was taken up in glory." In view of this verse and this Lesson, what emotions might the angels have experienced? _____

_____

_____

2. What do you notice about the timing of the angels' appearances in this Lesson? _____

_____

3. Why do you suppose there was so much demon activity during the Lord's ministry on earth? _____

_____

_____

4. In one sentence describe the role angels played in Jesus' earthly life: _____

_____

5. How well did God employ angels in the earthly life of Jesus?

_____

6. What does this tell you about them? _____

_____

7. What does it say about our heavenly Father? _____

_____

_____

Closing Prayer

Our God and Father, how can we ever sufficiently thank You for all You have done for us by giving us Your Son to be our Savior? Dear Lord Jesus, You created the holy angels and throughout the Old Testament they carried out Your orders. We praise You for their ministry to You as the divine plan of redemption unfolded. The angels are not ashamed of You — Zechariah came close — give us grace to proudly stand up for You here on earth. The critical role which many of the

79

heavenly host played in Your ministry is becoming clearer to us. Praise to You, dear Father, for sending the angels at just the right time and for just the right task. Give us grace to declare the Good News of Jesus' birth, suffering, death, resurrection, and ascension to one another and especially to unbelievers. May we be people of prayer in the hour of temptation. Refresh us daily through Your Word. May we glory in the death and resurrection of our dear Savior. May we look forward to the day that we, too, leave this earth to ascend up to heaven and we are received by You because of the merits of our Savior, Jesus Christ. Thank You, Father, for this Story of Angels from Your Holy Word. We are refreshed. To You, O God, be glory and honor now and forever and ever! In Jesus' name! Amen.

Closing Hymn

The holy apostolic band
Upon the Mount of Olives stand.
Alleluia, alleluia!
And with His faithful foll'wers see
Their Lord ascend in majesty.
Alleluia, alleluia! Alleluia, alleluia, alleluia!

To whom two shining angels cry,
"Why stand and gaze upon the sky?"
Alleluia, alleluia!
"This is the Savior," thus they say;
"This is His glorious triumph day!"
Alleluia, alleluia! Alleluia, alleluia, alleluia!

Give us your joy on earth, O Lord,
In heav'n to be our great reward,
Alleluia, alleluia!
Where, throned with You forever, we
Shall praise Your name eternally.
Alleluia, alleluia! Alleluia, alleluia, alleluia!

THE STORY OF ANGELS

Evil Angels Today

Opening Hymn

Crown Him with many crowns, The Lamb upon His throne;
Hark how the heav'nly anthem drowns All music but its own.
Awake, my soul and sing Of Him who died for thee,
And hail Him as thy matchless King Through all eternity.

Crown Him the Lord of love, behold His hands and side,
Rich wounds, yet visible above, In beauty glorified.
No angels in the sky Can fully bear that sight,
But downward bend their wondering eyes At mysteries so bright.

Can you remember the most terrifying dream you have ever had? I can. It happened just as I began research on this particular Bible study. In my dream I saw a little girl standing in the street. Suddenly, in the high bushes by a house across the street, there was a huge commotion and a calf with the head of a devil came out of the bushes. It streaked across the street, hitting the little girl who fell to the ground, and she turned into a dead dog. The calf disappeared. I awoke and was terrified, so much so that I could not go back to sleep and was afraid of sharing the details with my wife. Friend, we have a great need today. We need to be more aware of the attacks of Satan and the evil angels on people everywhere before the end comes.

One example: Alabama Federal Judge Ira De Ment has commanded that student-led prayer is forbidden in the schools, that student commencement speakers can make only a passing reference to God and cannot ask anyone in the audience to join in prayer. The judge has threatened students and school officials with disciplinary action if they disobey the order. Prayer is even forbidden in a time of national emergency including war. Her order also established undercover school monitors to watch for any violations. The Governor has called the monitors "secret police." Just a glance around this old world tells you that Satan and his evil angels are alive and well.

Warning

Iraqi terrorist, Khay Rahnajet, didn't pay enough postage on a letter bomb. It came back with "return to sender" stamped on it. You guessed it, he opened it! While on the one hand the evil spirits are dumb (who would ever try to throw the Lord out of heaven?), yet they are also very smart. What warnings do the following verses have for God's children?

1. 1 Timothy 4:1 _____

_____

2. John 8:44 _____

_____

3. 2 Corinthians 11:13-15 _____

_____

4. 1 John 4:1 _____

_____

● DO NOT WORSHIP

1. Paul speaks against angel worship when he says, "Do not let anyone who delights in false humility and the *worship of angels* disqualify you for the prize" (Colossians 2:18).

666

The number given to the devil in Revelation 13:18

2. What did John do and how was he corrected twice?

    Revelation 19:10 _____

_____

Revelation 22:8-9 _____

_____

3. True or False: The sight and sound of a holy angel must be beyond our present understanding or anything we can even imagine. This may just be one reason why angels are usually invisible to us. If I heard and saw an angel as John did, I, too, might be tempted to fall down and worship him.

● **DECEIVING SIGNS AND WONDERS**

1. Read 2 Thessalonians 2:9-10a. What is Satan capable of doing?

_____

2. True or False: The signs and wonders are astonishing, but they are still a deception, a lie; nevertheless, the signs and wonders do deceive those who are perishing. Defend your answer (One key word in v. 9 will help you).

● **GOD OF THIS AGE**

1. Read 2 Corinthians 4:4. The Devil is the god of this age because he is the embodiment of all the wickedness in this world. One of his worst activities is mentioned. What is it? _____

_____

What is the result? _____

2. Many a sinner has been clearly told of God's love for him, of a free salvation by faith alone in the Savior and which is a gift from God, yet the sinner continues to think of the Gospel as if it were nothing. The Bible further tells man clearly about the Devil, and man treats the Devil as a joke. Who is responsible? _____

The Occult

Playing games with the Devil can appear to be rather innocent, but yet, very deadly. A closer look reveals why.

● **DIVINATION**

1. Let's get a solid definition of divination.

> Divination, the art of obtaining secret knowledge, especially of the future, is a pagan counterpart of prophecy. Careful comparison of Scripture will reveal that inspirational divination is by demonic power... Seeking knowledge of the future from any source other than the God of Israel was an insult to His holy Being and the revelation of Himself and His purpose for men (*The New Unger's Bible Dictionary*, p. 313, by Merrill F. Unger).

This stands in direct contrast to the Lord who permitted prophets to speak of future events such as the coming Messiah. These are revelations from God. Divination is a tool of the Devil.

2. Note that Satan's knowledge of the future is limited; he can make guesses; he cannot control them. What is the Lord's challenge in Isaiah 41:22-24? _____

_____

What is the Lord's conclusion? _____

_____

3. How were people making a lot of money through a diviner in Acts 16:16-18? _____

How was it brought to an end? _____

4. What is the Lord's advice in Isaiah 8:19? _____

_____

5. What does God expressly forbid in Deuteronomy 18:9-11? _____

_____

_____

Leviticus 20:27 tells us how great a sin divination is in the sight of God: "'A man or woman who is a *medium* or *spiritist* among you must be put to death. You are to stone them; their blood will be on their own heads.'"

- **ASTROLOGY**

Astrology is very popular today, and it is divination. More than 1,000 newspapers in America carry the horoscope. Many Christians were shocked to learn that Nancy Reagan consulted regularly with astrologer Joan Quigley, and we discovered that many of the President's meetings were planned according to the stars. Some people claim that astrology is a science, but it is anything but. Many horoscopes seem

to offer nothing more than common sense: "Be careful when you are driving today. Do not take any chances on losing money. Stay away from negative people." That sort of advice is good every day. Where did astrology come from? The Babylonians. It appears that Babylon used astrology more than any other nation in history.

Read Isaiah 47:13-14. What is the result of frantically seeking answers from things like astrology according to 13a? _____

What does God compare astrologers and stargazers to? _____

_____ God asked Job: "Can you bind the beautiful Pleiades? Can you loose the cords of Orion? Can you bring forth the constellations in their seasons or lead out the bear with its cubs? Do you know the laws of the heavens? Can you set up [God's] dominion over the earth?" (38:31-33). The answer is "No!" Our strength and hope for the present and future does not rest in man, but in God. It is not found in the stars, but on the cross of Calvary where Jesus said, "It is finished!" He calls us His sons and daughters and promises that He will return soon to take us Home.

- **GAMES**

"Dungeons & Dragons" is a popular game bearing the occult theme, and it promotes demons, dragons and creatures who can give spells and have super-power. Players get out of the dungeon any way they can: killing, raping, and casting spells. It is said that it is only imaginary, but it introduces people to occult thinking, rituals, and names.

The Ouija board has been around for many years and has been

very popular. It uses the alphabet and the numbers 0 to 9, and the words "yes," "no," and "good bye." You ask a question, concentrate very hard, and wait for the answer to appear. The manufacturers call it a "mystifying oracle," and say that it is just a fun game. It, too, has been a stepping stone for many people into more serious forms of the occult. St. Paul's advice is excellent: "Finally, brothers, whatever is true, whatever is noble, whatever is right, whatever is pure, whatever is lovely, whatever is admirable — if anything is excellent or praiseworthy — think about such things" (Philippians 4:8).

Witchcraft

Witchcraft has been around for a long time. There are an estimated 10,000 practicing witches in North America. They have one thing in common — they have yielded themselves to the "rulers of darkness."

Not long ago I just spoke to my son, John, in Denver. He said he recently met a woman who claimed she was a witch, but, she told him, "I am a good witch." That is a claim which I believe all modern witches make. Today witches call their practice "The Craft," "Wica," Wicca," or "Benevolent Witchcraft." They see the divine in every human, tree, stream, rock, animal or any other form of nature. All witches seem to be unified in their worship of nature and the earth.

What does Paul call these people in Romans 1:22-23,25? _____

Why? _____

True or False: Witchcraft is paganism, plain and simple.

I made the suggestion to John, "Hey, stay away from that woman!" He said, "Don't worry. She was killed in an automobile accident shortly after I met her." What is the final end of people like this? Revelation 21:8 says, "But the cowardly, the unbelieving, the vile, the murderers, the sexually immoral, *those who practice magic arts*, the idolaters and all liars — their place will be in the fiery lake of burning sulfur. This is the second death."

Mormonism

Satan is still active today in many cults and sects. A perfect example of this is Mormonism. Joseph Smith founded the Mormon Church on

April 6, 1830. He said that an angel named Moroni appeared to him. His room was flooded with light. The angel was sent by God. Smith was told to restore the Gospel prior to the coming of the Messiah. The angel told Smith that there were plates of gold on which were engravings, and they were located in the Town of Manchester, Ontario County, N.Y. From this came the *Book of Mormon* in 1830.

Brigham Young succeeded Smith and made the Mormon Church what it is today. Mormonism believes more than ever that God uses angels to reveal new truth to His people. Mormons have thirteen Articles of Faith which, among other things, state: "We believe the Book of Mormon to be the Word of God. We believe that through the atonement of Christ all mankind may be saved by obedience to the laws and ordinances of the Gospel. We believe that God will yet reveal many great and important things pertaining to the kingdom of God."

1. What "red flags" do you see in these three sentences? _____

   _____

   _____

2. St. Paul had a very blunt statement to make about paganism in 1 Corinthians 10:19-20. What is it? _____

   _____

3. What warning does St. Paul have in Galatians 1:6-8? _____

   _____

New Age

New Age thought can be found in all arenas of life: eastern religions, psychology, ecology, entertainment, education, medicine, and in many main stream denominations in America. What is this new religion? Basically it centers on self. Shirley MacLaine has written a number of books on the subject. For example, she writes, "Each soul is its own

God. You must never worship anyone or anything other than self. For you are God. To love self is to love God" (*Dancing in the Light*, p. 385, by Shirley MacLaine). They consider God to be the seen and the unseen universe.

New Age has also accelerated interest in angels who give them insights to better living. There is no distinction between holy and evil angels. While the Bible declares that man was terrified on actually seeing a holy angel, New Age presents angels as pussycats, soft, cuddly, feminine, totally non-threatening. Nancy Gibbs made this accurate statement: "Only in the New Age would it be possible to invent an angel so mellow that it can be ignored" (*Time*, December, 1993). Now that is truly non-threatening.

1. Why do you suppose people, including religious people, are so turned on by this type of angel? _____

_____

2. What most important thing, more important than anything else, is missing in today's angel craze? _____

3. The holy angels in the Bible seem to always point people to _____ whereas the New Age angel points people to _____ From our study so far we can rightly conclude that the Devil never looks like _____

Christine Joy Staber was brought up by loving parents and faithfully attended a conservative Lutheran Church and then got involved in the "New Age." Read her story, underline those parts which you think are important, and then discuss them informally.

In my own way I rebelled in the late 60's and 70's. I frequented beer parties and bars. I started to live by the accepted rules of the world and my own selfish motives which nearly destroyed my life. Because of the mess I made of my life I was an angry person — angry at God, myself, and life. I thought much about the purpose of life, and I did try a Lutheran Church here or there, but never heard about sin, repentance and the need of a Savior — just nice sermons.

One day (in the 1980's), while watching the Oprah Winfrey Show, I listened to Shirley MacLaine express her belief in Eastern religions, reincarnation and extraterrestrials. Ms. MacLaine's books entered my home and there I began a downward spiral into the hands of Satan. Her books quoted many authors. Those books also entered my home. Some of the more dangerous books were by Edgar Cayce. An American psychic renowned for his trance readings, he promoted reincarnation and karma. He is known as the "father of the New Age Movement."

The newsletters of his organization, "Association for Research and Enlightenment," entered my home. I began to frequent occult bookstores and the occult section of my local public library, and occult books started to enter my home. I attended a seminar conducted by Edgar Cayce's grandson, Hugh Lynn Cayce, and was fully exposed to the philosophy of the "New Age."

But surprisingly this is when I began to ask questions. I knew my Mom was praying for me. I often recalled her reading from *Portals of Prayer* and the Scripture at our evening meal. I read about the King James Bible and its accuracy and decided I needed a new Bible. I visited a Christian bookstore and with a book called *Life In Christ* and the Scriptures as my teacher, I became a born again child of God in May of 1987.

I read through the Bible my first year and the next several years. I prayed and searched the Scriptures. I was consumed with the Word.

The occult books that I had accumulated still lined my bookshelves. Each time I walked by them it seemed evident to me by a gentle touch that I should remove these books. I boxed them up and put them in the basement of my house. This was okay for a while, but eventually the same gentle touch occurred, and I knew these books needed to leave my house, which they did.

My eyes were opened, and I saw how "New Age" philosophy had permeated our world. With intensified awareness I started to share my testimony with others. I started to write articles to expose the "New Age" and occasionally spoke to women's groups.

This next part is hard for me to understand. I began to be aware of a presence in my home — mostly in the hallway at the landing of the steps leading to my bedroom (the room where I accepted Jesus into my heart). "It" was present but not a part of me, but I was aware that this was what "it" wanted. How do I describe this presence? I was aware "it" was very evil. "Its" appearance was that of consuming wickedness. "It" had no real appearance (bodily), but "it" sometimes seemed to manifest "itself" with a face that consisted of unspeakable evil, eyes full of wickedness and hatred and the ability to hurt and harm, a mouth contorted with sarcasm and taunting, that seemed to mock and ridicule. I knew that this presence was enticing me to give in to "it" (he seemed male, but I don't know), to return to the darkness I once knew or at least not deal with "its" presence. "It" seemed to tempt, oppress, harass and cause me to question and accuse me: "Are your sins really forgiven?", "Remember all the depravity of your former self?", "Surely Jesus' sacrifice on the cross could never undo your sins!"

I would plead with God in my prayer time to hang on to me. I would literally hold out my hand towards Him and ask Him to hold so very, very tight that I could never go back to the darkness even if I wanted to.

This "presence" would terrify me daily. Then one afternoon I sat down in the very area where "it" seemed to be. I folded my hands in prayer and said: "In the Name of Jesus, my Lord and Savior, I tell you to depart from this place. I hate you. I hate everything about you. I belong to Jesus Christ. You have no power over me. Depart from this place in the Name of Jesus Christ!"

"It" left. I got up knowing that my God is a powerful God, and my soul rested.

I don't understand what the presence was all about or even why God allowed it. Perhaps it was because, as former New Ager Randall Baer wrote: "Satan does not let go easily of those he has had in his grip, who have escaped by the Victory of Jesus."

Perhaps it was to help me understand how totally evil Satan is, that what I once thought was enlightenment was really the darkness and wickedness of Satan and outright rebellion against God, and that when that deceptive light is exposed by the true Light it cannot withstand the power and the presence and the majesty of Jesus.

I love You Jesus!

Christine Joy Staber
Christ Lutheran Church, Chippewa Falls, WI

Demon Possession

We read in Luke 22:3, "Then *Satan* entered Judas, called Iscariot, one of the Twelve." This was stealing a soul, not demon possession. Satan promotes false teaching (1 Timothy 4:1-2), but that is not possession. 1 Samuel 16:14 says, "Now the Spirit of the LORD had departed from Saul, and an *evil spirit* from the LORD tormented him." The Lord allowed Satan to afflict Job. He also allowed an evil spirit to enter Saul. While we cannot prove that this was demon possession, it would seem that it was actual possession.

> Jesus treated cases of demonic possession as realities. He is not only described as "rebuking," "commanding," and "casting out" the unclean spirits, but His direct addresses to them are recorded... He deliberately argued with the Jews on the assumption of the reality of demonic possession, affirming that His casting out demons by the Spirit of God proved that the kingdom of God had come to them (Matt. 12:23-28; Luke 11:14-26)... We are further informed (Mark 3:14-15) that in the solemn act of calling and appointing the apostles "He appointed twelve, that they might be with Him, and that He might send them out to preach, and to have authority to cast out demons." Clearly demonism was regarded by our Lord as a stern reality (*The New Unger's Bible Dictionary*, p. 298, by Merrill F. Unger).

During our Savior's public ministry demon possession reached epidemic proportions. Demon possession still occurs today, but not at that level.

1. Read Mark 5:1-20. Here is a classic example of demon possession. How did the demons show their power? _____

    _____

    Their knowledge? _____

    How did the Lord show His power? _____

    Why did the people ask Jesus to leave? _____

    _____

    What did the healed man do? _____

2. True or False: As a Christian I cannot be demon possessed today (1 John 4:4). Defend your answer: _____

3. Where do you suppose we got the idea that the demons are stronger than we are? _____

Near Death Experiences

Spiritism (talking to departed spirits) was practiced in the Old Testament. There is a new kind of spiritism among us today, and it is called near-death experiences. It is interesting to note that unbelievers and believers both report going through a tunnel and then seeing a warm, bright light.

1. Are these experiences equal or superior to Scriptural teaching on what happens after death? _____

It is important to compare their "experiences" to God's Holy Word. Both Paul and John were "taken up" to heaven, but their reports, guided by the Holy Spirit, are very different from what we read about today. Remember the story of the rich man and Lazarus in Luke 16:19-31? When the rich man was in hell he asked Abraham to bring Lazarus back to life and that he might go to his unbelieving brothers so that, upon seeing Lazarus, they might repent and believe. The rich man said (Luke 16:30), "But if someone from the dead goes to them, they will repent." Abraham replied (Luke 16:31), "If they do not listen to Moses and the Prophets, they will not be convinced even if someone rises from the dead." The Bible gives us all the proof we need about life after death and how to get ready for it. In Isaiah 8:19 we told, "Why consult the dead on behalf of the living?"

2. What dangers do you see when people give near-death experiences priority over Scripture? _____

_____

_____

Our Victory

I read where the average cost of rehabilitating a seal after the Exxon

92

Valdez oil spill in Alaska was $80,000. At a special ceremony two of the most expensively saved animals were released back into the wild amid cheers and applause from onlookers. A minute later they were both eaten by a killer whale. That was anything but a victory for the environmentalists and government officials present. What a waste. We Christians, on the other hand, do not spin our wheels like that.

Despite the numbers and power of demons today, our victory is positively assured. It is assured because of Jesus. "And having disarmed the *powers and authorities*, He made a public spectacle of them, triumphing over them by the cross" (Colossians 2:15). The cross is God's definitive answer to the question of our sin and Satan. In Matthew 12:22-30 Jesus refers to Himself as One who drives out demons. Before Him demons flee. Through Him we have the victory. We won't, but all demons and all unbelievers will be swallowed up by something much worse than a killer whale.

Read Revelation 12:10-11. The accuser is _____ , but he has been hurled _____ How do those who overcome win the victory? _____

_____

In the meantime, we will be careful. "Dear friends, do not believe *every spirit*, but test the spirits to see *whether they are from God*, because many false prophets have gone out into the world" (1 John 4:1). Look carefully at the following advice from Scripture.

- KNOW SATAN'S SCHEMES

2 Corinthians 2:10-11 is interesting. "If you forgive anyone, I also forgive him. And what I have forgiven — if there was anything to forgive — I have forgiven in the sight of Christ for your sake, in order that *Satan* might *not outwit* us. For we are not unaware of his *schemes*." Satan was not just seeking the downfall of one individual, rather, he was scheming to drive a wedge between the Corinthians and Paul which would result in even more damage. We, too, need to be alert to the evil

93

schemes of Satan in our private lives, in our families, in our church, and wherever there are fellow believers.

- **PURSUE THE TRUTH**

1. Read 2 Thessalonians 2:9-10. Every believer needs to remember two sets of truths for victory over the Devil. First, he needs to be careful

    about _____ and second, and

    even more important, he needs to love _____

    What is meant by the second statement? _____

    _____

2. Read Matthew 4:1-4. How did Jesus survive the vicious temptations

    of the Devil? _____

    What are the implications of Jesus' answer for you on a daily basis?

    _____

    _____

- **RESIST HIM**

1. Satan is the prime promoter and exploiter of lying and anger. It's a problem for all of us, but St. Paul says: "Do not give the devil a *foothold*" (Ephesians 4:27). What does this mean for everyday living

    as you face anger or even the threat of it? _____

    _____

    When you do this, does it help? _____

2. Would you like to defeat the Devil more frequently? _____
    James 4:7 says, "*Submit* yourselves, then, to God. *Resist* the devil, and he will flee from you" (4:7). In verse 6 James says, "God opposes the *proud* but gives grace to the *humble*." Follow this plan decisively and you will defeat the Devil. What do you do? Get rid of your *pride!*

    Get *humble!* Then you are ready to _____ yourself to

    God, and then you are ready to _____ the

    Devil. And what is the final result? _____

94

Have you tried these four steps? _____ What happened?

_____

What are you learning here? _____

_____

- **STAND FIRM**

You can read about the daily successes of the demons on the front page of your newspaper. Here is more critical advice for you from the Lord.

1. Read 1 Peter 5:8-9. Write verbs which tell what you are to do:

    _____

2. Read Ephesians 6:11-17. List the equipment you need to wear and

    use: _____

    _____

Concluding Thoughts

1. True or False: I believe that many times a demon whispers evil things in my one ear and an angel whispers good things in the other ear. Defend your answer.

2   True or False: You can be sure that the Devil never really looks like the Devil. Defend your answer.

3. True or False: Divination, astrology, and games like the Ouija board are perfectly harmless. Defend your answer.

4. How would you answer a person who says, "We really should be more concerned about things that we can see than things we

    cannot see."? _____

    _____

5. True or False: "The Devil made me do it." Technically, I could say that only if I were demonized. Otherwise I may have to say, "The Devil encouraged me, and I fell for his lies and deception."

Closing Prayer

Dear Lord Jesus, we thank You that You have loved us so much and that in Your earthly ministry You demonstrated how it is possible to win victory after victory over the prince of darkness and his demons. We pray for all those people who today are held in the tight grip of the evil one. Have mercy on them, dear Lord. Pour out Your Holy Spirit upon them and bring them the saving Gospel. We ask for Your intervention in our lives. Keep us from sin and shame. Do not let us believe every spirit, but may we test them and judge them according to Your Word. May we be alert to Satan's schemes in our private lives, in our families, in our church, and wherever there are fellow believers. Lord, move us to a daily study of Your holy Word at home, to hear it preached in our worship services each Sunday, and to study it each week with other Christians in Bible study groups. Forgive us where we have failed You. We submit ourselves to You, and we earnestly desire to dress ourselves up in the spiritual armament and clothing at our disposal. Lord, keep us in our hour of temptation. So fill our hearts with Your love that we will do all in our power to reach out to unbelieving people everywhere that they may come to know You as their Lord and Savior. We ask this in Your powerful name. Amen.

Closing Hymn

Stand up, stand up for Jesus, Stand in His strength alone;
The arm of flesh will fail you, you dare not trust your own.
Put on the Gospel armor, Each piece put on with prayer;
Where duty calls, or danger Be never wanting there.

Stand up, stand up for Jesus, The strife will not be long;
This day the noise of battle, The next the victor's song.
To him that overcometh A crown of life shall be:
He with the King of glory Shall reign eternally.

Lesson 9

THE STORY OF ANGELS

Angels and Believers Today

Opening Hymn

Nearer, my God, to Thee, Nearer to Thee.
E'en though it be a cross, That raiseth me,
Still all my song shall be, Nearer, my God, to Thee,
Nearer, my God, to Thee, Nearer to Thee.

There let my way appear Steps unto heav'n;
All that Thou sendest me In mercy giv'n;
Angels to beckon me Nearer, my God, to Thee,
Nearer, my God, to Thee, Nearer to Thee.

Have you ever seen an angel? Would you like to? Well, here are two differing approaches.

One way to attract angels is to wear the kinds of clothes they like. Wearing something that the angels will like is a personal choice based on your own perception and the idea of angels. Here are some ideas. Colors to wear to attract specific angels:
Guardians: rose or pine and soft green
Healing angels: deep sapphire blue
Angels of birth: sky blue
Ceremonial and music angels: white
The seraphim: crimson red
The cherubim: blue
Archangel Michael: deep green, vivid blue, gold, and rose
Archangel Gabriel: tans, browns, and greens.
Jasmine and rose are said to be noticeable when angels (especially guardian angels) are near. Pine is said to attract

97

healing angels, and its scent is noticeable when they are near" (*Messengers of Light*, pp. 118-119, by Terry Lynn Taylor).

In their book, *Ask Your Angels*, Daniel, Wyllie, and Rammer have this suggestion for angelic contact: "Aligning. This step brings the meditator in alignment with the angelic realm by expanding the senses. This can be done by listening to music, visualizing golden light, or chanting the following angel chant: 'Eee Nu Rah — Eee Nu Rah — Eee Nu Rah — Zay.'"

Do any of you in this study group want to try that now? No? All of us want to be nearer to God. A sister in Christ made this lament to me this morning: "A few of my friends have said they have seen angels, and when they ask me if I ever have, I just tell them 'No.'" Maybe you feel like that. This Lesson will help as we pursue "Angels and Believers Today."

Rejoicing

1. Read Luke 15:1-10. Who was the Lord speaking these parables to?

    _____ What was the one great

    glaring difference between them and the angels in heaven? _____

    _____

    Did the angels ever rejoice over them? _____

    Have they ever rejoiced over you? Why or why not? _____

    _____

    True or False: From these parables it would be safe to assume that
    angels watch what goes on in a sinner's heart.

2. The angels are awesome in many ways, yet they cannot experience conversion to the Lord Jesus Christ as their personal Savior. Why, then, do you suppose that the angels are so happy over the conversion

    of a single unbeliever? _____

98

What might be the significance of their doing this in the presence of God? _____

Why should their rejoicing impact on us? _____

What difference should it make in our lives today? _____

Watching

1. How would your daily living be affected if you knew that angels were constantly watching you? _____

   Paul tells Timothy, "I charge you, in the *sight* of God and Christ *Jesus* and the *elect angels*, to keep these instructions without partiality, and to do nothing out of favoritism" (1 Timothy 5:21). Paul is telling Timothy to be aware of the fact that not only the Lord, but also the holy angels are watching him. He is to conduct his daily living accordingly. Why do you suppose we do not seem to pay much attention to this admonition, at least as it applies to the

   angels watching us? _____

2. Again St. Paul writes, "For it seems to me that God has put us apostles on *display* at the end of the procession, like men condemned to die in the arena. We have been made a *spectacle* to the whole universe, to *angels* as well as to men" (1 Corinthians 4:9). What Paul said about the apostles being seen by men and angels would also apply to all believers of all time. What effect should this have on your daily living this week and every week?

   What should be the prime motivating factor for our living properly for the Lord? _____

Guarding

1. Read the following two articles carefully.

When you are in a dentist's chair, ask for the Angel of Fearlessness to be with you. Perhaps an Angel of Strength and an Angel of Patience, or an Angel of Calmness. For the dentist, ask for Angels of Steadiness, Swiftness, Painlessness, and Wisdom to guide his hands. Ask for anything you want to have happen, and an angel will be there immediately to blend with your personal energy (*Angelspeak*, p. 25, by Barbara Mark and Trudy Griswold).

The Rev. John G. Paton, missionary in the New Hebrides Islands, tells the thrilling story involving the protective care of angels. Hostile natives surrounded his mission headquarters one night, intent on burning the Patons out and killing them. John Paton and his wife prayed all during that terror-filled night that God would deliver them. When daylight came they were amazed to see the attackers unaccountably leave. They thanked God for delivering them.

A year later, the chief of the tribe was converted to Jesus Christ, and Mr. Paton, remembering what had happened, ask the chief what kept him and his men from burning down the house and killing them. The chief replied in surprise, "Who were all those men you had with you there?" The missionary answered, "There were no men there; just my wife and I." The chief argued that they had seen many men standing guard — hundreds of big men in shining garments with drawn swords in their hands. They seemed to circle the mission station so that the natives were afraid to attack. Only then did Mr. Paton realize that God had sent His angels to protect them. The chief agreed that there was no other explanation. Could it be that God had sent a legion of angels to protect His servants whose lives were being endangered (*Angels: God's Secret Agents*, p. 3, by Billy Graham)?

Which of these two articles seems unbelievable and why? _____

Which of these two articles seems believable and why? _____

_____

2. It would appear that angels do not minister to God's peoples' spiritual needs, with the exception of bringing a spiritual message from heaven to earth (Christmas to the shepherds), but rather they minister to the physical needs of God's people on earth.

Read Matthew 18:10. Jesus tells us not to look down on one of these little ones as though they were really not very important. Notice, do not look down on even one of them! Perhaps the Lord was looking into the future when those in the church would be tempted to neglect the small ones. "I tell you" means that Jesus is using His authority in giving this command. "Their angels," that is, the angels watching over them, "always see the face of My Father in heaven." This passage does not support the teaching that all children have guardian angels or that every human being is assigned a guardian angel at birth. God, however, assigns individual angels to these children to care for them. If the angels delight in doing this, shall not those of us who are adults do the same? The answer is yes!

Phillipp Melanchthon wrote —

> For angels never rest nor sleep as we;
> Their whole delight is but to be
> With You, Lord Jesus, and to keep
> Your little flock, Your lambs and sheep.

True or False: From Matthew 18:10 we can conclude that all believers, no matter what their age, have guardian angels.

3. Read Hebrews 1:14. The angels are called spirits, without bodies, possessing entity, superb intelligence, wisdom, and strength. What

is the function of the angels according to this verse? _____

_____

True or False: This verse does not assign a Christian one angel, but simply indicates that any number of angels may be commissioned by God to serve His people.

101

4. Should we pray to these angels? _____

_____

Prayer to One's Guardian Angel

Angel of God, my guardian dear, to whom his love commits me here, ever this day (night) be at my side, to light and guard, to rule and guide. Amen (*The Essential Catholic Handbook,* p. 73).

Why would you not want to pray this prayer to an angel? _____

_____

_____

5. If you were in great danger, which would you prefer — having one guardian angel or having thousands of them helping you? Why?

_____

_____

6. The Scriptures repeatedly verify the protective ministry of God's angels to all of us. And sometimes it may be in a less dramatic way. A pastor exclaimed to another pastor on greeting him, "Wow! I almost had a horrible accident on the way to the conference. My car was nearly broadsided! But God's holy angels were with me and my life was spared!" "That's not so unusual," said the other pastor. "Absolutely nothing happened to me on the way to the conference" (*The Truth About Angels,* p. 19, by Donald L. Deffner)!

How do you explain what happened? _____

_____

_____

7. Have you ever been in serious danger and, yet, were not hurt?

_____ Did it occur to you that angels may have

delivered you? _____

Have you gone through life with few or no apparent dangers around? _____ Did it occur to you that angels may have been protecting you? _____

8. Would you rather see or not see these angels who guard you? Why?

_____

_____

9. Mention some things your guardian angel(s) would not do: _____

_____

_____

_____

Delivering

Ole and Lena had a terrible marriage. A day never went by without bad words between the two; in fact, they downright hated each other. One day Ole died and stood before Peter at the gate to heaven. Ole said, "Peter, can I come in?" Peter said, "You can come in if you can spell one word correctly for me." Ole said, "Okay. What is the word?" Peter said, "Spell 'God.'" Ole said, "G-o-d." "Good," said Peter. "You can come in." A few days later Peter asked Ole if he would watch the gate because he had some other things to take care of. Ole agreed. At this very time Lena died. She stood at the gate and said, "Ole, can I come in to heaven?" Ole said, "Sure, but first you have to spell one word correctly for me." "Okay," said Lena, "what is the word?" Ole said, "Albuquerque!"

Thanks to Jesus, our dear Savior, we don't get into heaven on our spelling. And thanks to the holy angels, we don't have to worry about the trip or even about standing at the gate to get in. It is the trip that we're concerned about here and the role angels play in it.

Jude 9: "Even the archangel Michael, when he was disputing with the devil about the body of Moses, did not dare to bring a slanderous accusation against him." The body of Moses, you might know, vanished after his death. God took him, we are told in the Old Testament, and personally buried him in Moab

(Dt. 34:5-6). For some reason, which may have had to do with the prophetic reappearance of Moses before the coming of the Lord, there was a heated dispute between Michael and Satan over possession of the body of Moses. We cannot know with certainty why Satan wanted Moses' cadaver, but one thing is clear: angels, dark and light, were hovering around his deathbed.

Angels appear on the edge of death because death is the threshold between time and eternity. Death is a room with a view beyond the veil. In the Bible, nearly every encounter with heaven — visions, dreams, miracles, revelations about the future, the Second Coming of Christ and the Day of Judgment — is enveloped in the presence of angels. If death is the door to eternity, angels are the doormen (*Angels Dark and Light*, pp. 100-101, by Gary Kinnaman).

1. Read Luke 16:22. The rich man and Lazarus were very different

   before _____ and even more different after _____.

   _____ came at death and carried the soul of Lazarus

   to "Abraham's side" — that was a picture to the Jew of the feasting and happiness we'll have in heaven. The angels were not just with

   Lazarus on the trip Home, but they actually _____ him.

2. Acts 1:9 reads, "After He said this, He was taken up before their very eyes, and a cloud hid Him from their sight." Luke 24:51 reads, "While He was blessing them, He left them and was taken up into heaven." Many Christians believe that angels took Jesus back to heaven. What words from these two verses allow for that

   opinion? _____

3. The Christian should never consider death a tragedy. Rather he should see it as the angels do: They realize that joy should mark the journey from time to eternity. The way to life is by the valley of death, but the road is marked with victory all the way. Angels revel in the power of the resurrection of Jesus, which assures us of our resurrection and guarantees us a safe passage to heaven.

   Hundreds of accounts record the heavenly escort of angels at death. When my maternal grandmother died, for instance, the room seemed to fill with a heavenly light. She sat up in bed and almost laughingly said, "I see Jesus. He has His arms outstretched for me. I see Ben [her husband who had died some years earlier] and I see the angels." She slumped over, absent from the body but present with the Lord (*Angels: God's Secret Agents*, p. 151-152, by Billy Graham).

4. Isaac Watts wrote —

> Lord! when I leave this mortal ground,
> And Thou shalt bid me rise and come,
> Send a beloved angel down,
> Safe to convey my spirit home!

Concluding Thoughts

1. If a holy angel appeared to you and gave you a message from God, would you be more elated over the message or in getting to see a holy angel? _____

   What do authors of many popular angel books stress today? ____

   _____

   What is going on? _____

2. Why the warning in Colossians 2:18? _____

   _____

3. True or False: As a believer you should know that angels are guarding you even when "bad things" happen to you.

4. True or False: It is okay to pray to angels if you believe in Jesus as your Savior.

5. Read Psalm 116. What are some feelings about death that you, as a child of God, should have? _____

   _____

   _____

   What comfort do you find in v. 15? _____

Closing Prayer

Lord God, You are the fountain of all blessing. We give glory to You for the holy angels. It is so wonderful that our conversion brought joy not only to You, but to all the angels in Your presence. Teach us to rejoice when we see sinners repent and believe. May we be more eager than ever to share the Good News with our unbelieving friends. We know that You watch us day by day, but it is also interesting to us that the angels do the same. We thank You for all those times when You sent angels to protect and keep us. Even though we cannot see them, we know that You continue to put angels beside us for our well-being. We look forward to the day when You will send the angels to carry us Home to be with You. A thousand thanks be to You for telling us about the angels. Lord, we want to see You! We long to be in Your presence! Help us keep our eyes focused on You. In Your name. Amen.

Closing Hymn

I am Jesus' little lamb, Ever glad at heart I am;
For my Shepherd gently guides me,
Knows my need and well provides me;
Loves me ev'ry day the same, Even calls me by my name.

Day by day, at home, away, Jesus is my staff and stay.
When I hunger, Jesus feeds me,
Into pleasant pastures leads me;
When I thirst, He bids me go Where the quiet waters flow.

Who so happy as I am, Even now the Shepherd's lamb?
And when my short life is ended,
By His angel host attended,
He shall fold me to His breast, There within His arms to rest.

THE STORY OF ANGELS

On
Judgment Day
and Forever

Opening Hymn

Lo, He comes with clouds descending,
Once for favored sinners slain;
All the many saints attending
Swell the triumph of His train:
Alleluia! Alleluia! God appears on earth to reign.

Every eye shall now behold Him,
Robed in awesome majesty;
Those who once denied and killed Him,
Pierced and nailed Him to the tree,
Deeply wailing, deeply wailing,
Shall the true Messiah see.

A little boy was sleeping at his grandmother's house one night when he heard the grandfather clock strike thirteen. He ran out of the room into his grandmother's room and said, "Grandma, grandma! It's later than it's ever been before!" Yes it is! Yes it is! According to Bible reckoning, the world is only about six and a half thousand years old, yet, two thousand years ago the Holy Spirit moved His servant Peter to write: "The end of all things is *near*" (1 Peter 4:7). Further we are told, "God has *set a day* when He will judge the world with justice by the Man (that's Jesus) He has appointed" (Acts 17:31).

For centuries believers have been waiting for the Lord to come back as He promised. Men have made many predictions about the Last Day, and they have all proven false. But while man does not know the date, one would think that the angelic hosts would. The hosts of heaven are so close to God and seem to know so much, but our Lord tells us an amazing fact: "No one knows about that day or hour, *not even the angels* in heaven, nor the Son, but only the Father" (Matthew 24:36).

We get a preview of this Day from John. Read Revelation 19:11-16. How do these words describe the appearance of the Lord on this Day?

Angels were very active during the earthly ministry of our Lord. They are even more active at the end of time. We see the word "angel" more than sixty times in the Book of Revelation.

Introducing the Day

A young girl, dressed in her Sunday best, was running as fast as she could to Sunday School. As she ran, she prayed, "Dear Lord, please don't let me be late! Dear Lord, please don't let me be late!" — at which moment she tripped on a curb and fell, getting her clothes dirty and tearing her dress. She got up, brushed herself off, and started running again, praying, "Dear Lord, please don't let me be late! Dear Lord, please don't let me be late! — but don't shove me!" No one is going to be late for Judgment Day, no one! Even perpetual procrastinators will be on time. What will happen?

1. There is going to be something awesome to see! Look at this Old Testament prophecy: "Enoch, the seventh from Adam, prophesied about these men: 'See, the Lord is coming with *thousands upon thousands* of His *holy ones*'" (Jude 14). Jesus says, "When the Son of Man comes in His glory, and *all the angels* with Him, He will sit on His throne in heavenly glory" (Matthew 25:31). And St. Paul, "This will happen when the Lord Jesus is revealed from heaven in blazing fire with His *powerful angels*" (2 Thessalonians 1:7). The sky will be filled with angels who will surround the Lord — perhaps all the hosts of heaven will be included in this scene.

2. Read Matthew 24:30-31a. In Bible times the Jews were often called

 together by the sound of a trumpet. In times of peace the trumpet sounded softly. In times of war and calamity, it sounded loud. How do you suppose the trumpet call will sound on the Last Day? _____

Who is this trumpet call for? _____

What is the assembly for? _____

True or False: Gabriel will blow the trumpet.

2. Read 1 Thessalonians 4:16. What is the loud command? _____

_____

Who speaks it (John 5:28)? _____

Who rises first from the dead? _____

Dividing Believers from Unbelievers

1. How is the task of the angels described in:

Matthew 24:31? _____

_____

Matthew 13:38-41? _____

_____

2. The angels will not be confused or "in the dark" as to who is a believer and who is an unbeliever. What does this suggest about them? _____

Where will the angels place the sheep? _____

Where will they place the goats? _____

3. True or False: The angels will know if we belonged to a good church denomination like the one we belong to or a bad denomination in which there are no believers.

True or False: I may be surprised at some of the sheep in this group that I thought were really goats.

109

Execute Judgment

1. Darwin's troubles have just started and the same applies to all who reject the love of God in Christ Jesus. Hebrews 1:7 reads, "In speaking of the *angels* He says, 'He makes

> Seen on a bumper sticker:
> ## Darwin: God is dead!
> ## God: Darwin is dead!

His *angels winds,* His *servants flames of fire.*'" When God makes

His angels "winds" He is suggesting to us that they are _____
When He makes angels "flames of fire" He is suggesting to us that

they _____

2. A letter came from Health and Human Services to a resident of Greenville County, South Carolina: "Your food stamps will be stopped, effective March, 1992, because we received notice that you passed away. May God bless you. You may reapply if your circumstances change." No, they are not going to change. Here is a government worker who is trying to be thoughtful and, yet, knows nothing about death and judgment. There are two judgments. The first judgment is private and takes place at the moment of death and is irrevocable. The soul is either received into heaven or condemned to hell. The second judgment is public. It is called Judgment Day. How public will it be? It will be in the presence of all the holy angels and before all men who have ever lived.

3. Read Matthew 13:41-43, 49-50. The angels are under the direct

control of _____ What is the task of the

angels? _____

How does Jesus describe hell? _____

_____

True or False: We need to be careful not to use these terms today in sermons and in our personal talks with our unbelieving friends lest they be offended. Defend your answer.

True or False: Somewhere in my Christian life I have made it plain to an unbeliever that unbelief will be rewarded with the anguish of hell on the Last Day, and I have also made it plain that God greatly desires this person to repent and believe in Jesus and be saved.

4. True or False: It is the believer's job to share the Gospel with unbelievers, and it will be the angels' job to separate the unbelievers from the believers.

5. Henry Alford wrote —

> For the Lord our God shall come
> And shall take His harvest home,
> From His field shall in that day
> All offenses purge away,
> Give His angels charge at last
> In the fire the tares to cast
> But the fruitful ears to store
> In His garner evermore.

The Evil Angels

1. Someone sent me this clipping:

> No more fire and brimstone? No more unrepentant sinners roasting for all eternity? The Church of England recently decided there was no point in continuing to scare people. So it redefined hell. Out with the idea of agonized, screaming souls who spend the hereafter in a fiery, bottomless pit. The new definition states that hell is "the final and irrevocable choosing of that which is opposed to God so completely and so absolutely that the only end is total non-being."

In other words, you just stop existing. Good news, if it were true, for the Devil and all his followers.

Another clipping:

> It will be harder to get to Hell this year. During the summer, repair crews will reconstruct a 62-year-old bridge that serves the main road through Hell, Michigan, blocking traffic for three months. The road suffers damage each year when Hell freezes over.

That's hard to believe. There is, however, no such problem with the real Hell which at first was created for Satan and all his followers. The story of Satan and his followers is a sad story. Read carefully these words of the prophet:

> "Surely the day is coming; *it will burn like a furnace.* All the

111

arrogant and every evildoer will be stubble, and that day that is coming will *set them on fire,*" says the LORD Almighty (Malachi 4:1).

2. Read Jude 6. Who is the "he"? _____

    True or False: God has "chained" the devils to hell, and on the Last Day He will pull in the chain.

    Why are their chains called everlasting? _____

    _____

3. Read Revelation 20:10. How long will the fallen angels suffer in hell? _____

    What one word is used to describe how they will be brought to hell?

    _____

Holy Angels

- **GIVE GOD EVERLASTING SERVICE**

1. Read Psalm 103:20-21. What three things will these angels do now and will continue to do forever?

    _____
    _____
    _____

2. True or False: God uses these angels for various kinds of services because He needs them to accomplish He will.

3. What seems to be their primary service to the Lord? _____

    _____

- **GIVE GOD EVERLASTING PRAISE**

1. Study the following verses carefully looking for reasons WHY the angelic host praise the Lord and underline them.

112

Ascribe to the LORD, O mighty ones, ascribe to the LORD glory and strength. Ascribe to the LORD the glory due His name; worship the LORD in the splendor of His holiness (Psalm 29:1-2).

Praise the LORD. Praise the LORD from the heavens, praise Him in the heights above. Praise Him, all His angels, praise Him, all His heavenly hosts (Psalm 148:1-2).

Each of the four living creatures had six wings and was covered with eyes all around, even under his wings. Day and night they never stop saying: "Holy, holy, holy is the Lord God Almighty, who was, and is, and is to come" (Revelation 4:8).

Then I looked and heard the voice of many angels, numbering thousands upon thousands, and ten thousand times ten thousand. They encircled the throne and the living creatures and the elders. In a loud voice they sang: "Worthy is the Lamb, who was slain, to receive power and wealth and wisdom and strength and honor and glory and praise!" (Revelation 5:11-12).

All the angels were standing around the throne and around the elders and the four living creatures. They fell down on their faces before the throne and worshiped God, saying: "Amen! Praise and glory and wisdom and thanks and honor and power and strength be to our God for ever and ever. Amen!" (Revelation 7:11-12).

2. "Day and night they will never stop saying..." (Revelation 4:8). For all eternity the angels will not become weary in giving praise to the Lord. What does this suggest? _____

_____

_____

3. If the holy angels, as awesome as they are, give God praise night and day, what does this tell us about our worship life? _____

_____

Each person in the class give one wrong idea we have about worship that seems to hinder us in our worship: _____

Give at least one idea that would help us worship the Lord better:

_____

4. Obviously the angels have these Bible verses down pat. Study these words carefully and underline WHY the angels worship the Lord the way they do.

> The fear of the LORD is the beginning of wisdom, and knowledge of the Holy One is understanding (Proverbs 9:10).

> Then a voice came from the throne, saying: "Praise our God, all you His servants, you who fear Him, both small and great!" Then I heard what sounded like a great multitude, like the roar of rushing waters and like loud peals of thunder, shouting: "Hallelujah! For our Lord God Almighty reigns. Let us rejoice and be glad and give Him glory! For the wedding of the Lamb has come, and His bride has made herself ready. Fine linen, bright and clean, was given her to wear" (Fine linen stands for the righteous acts of the saints.) (Revelation 19:5-8).

How would these words and concepts enable us to vastly improve our worship life. Be specific: _____

_____

_____

True or False: Chances are we will be mesmerized by the worship of the angels in heaven and will not be able to take our eyes off them. Defend your answer.

HALLELUJAH

The angels cannot help but shout "Hallelujah!" What does that word mean? _____

Why do you suppose we have trouble **shouting** that word to the Lord? _____

114

Thomas Olivers wrote it all down —

> The whole triumphant host
> Give thanks to God on high.
> "Hail, Father, Son, and Holy Ghost!"
> They ever cry.
> Hail, Abr'am's God and mine!
> I join the heav'nly lays:
> All might and majesty are Thine
> And endless praise.

Our Privilege and Honor

1. Read Luke 12:8-9. To confess Christ is one of the cardinal aims of a Christian. The Greek word for "acknowledge" (ομολογησει) means to "to say the same thing" as someone else and to confess it openly. Confess what? Jesus Christ and everything identified with Him. Where? Jesus promises that if you _____

   _____ then He will confess you

   _____ What a privilege and honor for us to confess Jesus before our fellow men! And what a prospect to look forward to when Jesus will call your name and confess you as His very own before all the angels of heaven! And what will happen to those who are ashamed of Jesus and will not confess

   Him? _____

Joseph Grigg wrote —

> Ashamed of Jesus? Yes, I may
> When I've no guilt to wash away,
> No tear to wipe, no good to crave,
> No fear to quell, no soul to save.
>
> Till then — nor is my boasting vain —
> Till then I boast a Savior slain;
> And oh, may this my glory be,
> That Christ is not ashamed of me!

Christian friend, stand up for Jesus today. Confess the glory of His name — and hear Jesus confess you by name before His angels!

115

2. The Sadducees denied the resurrection of the body. This is part of Jesus' response to that denial: "When the dead rise, they will neither marry nor be given in marriage; *they will be like the angels* in heaven" (Mark 12:25). The angels do not  have bodies in heaven — we will have bodies after the resurrection. We will, however, have a distinct likeness to the angels. The angels do not have marriage and sex — neither will we in heaven. The number of angels is fixed; it will not be increased. The number of saints in heaven, after the resurrection, will also be fixed. For more information on this and related points, see the author's Bible study entitled, *The Many Wonders of Heaven.*

Concluding Thoughts

1. These are critical times for God's people on earth.

Never before have God's people needed the vision of the unseen things and the believing anticipation of them so much as in our days. The playthings of the dust are being made more and more attractive by the god of this age to blind the eyes of them that believe not. We are, too, in constant danger to lose sight of the unseen things, because faith's vision becomes dimmed through the materialism of our times. For all we know, we are facing the first streaks of the coming day-dawn; the morning star is about to rise (*The Angels of God*, p. 113, by A. C. Gaebelein).

Which sentence by Gaebelein strikes you as being very significant and tell why? _____

_____

2. Why do you suppose the angels are given so many important assignments on the Last Day? Briefly list them. _____

_____

_____

_____

3. Read Acts 6:8-15; 7:59-60. What was it that caused the members of the Sanhedrin to look so intently at Stephen? _____

Apparently Stephen's face had a supernatural radiance and light that was like the brightness on an angel's face. Which words tell how that was possible? _____

_____

The members of the Sanhedrin looked at Stephen and were astonished — but they were not moved to believe on the Lord Jesus.

True or False: This is a small example of how we will look to one another in heaven, not because of angels, but because of Jesus.

Where did Stephen learn how to pray like he did in 7:59-60? ____

_____

4. Some time ago I was visiting the dining room of the United States Senate. As I was speaking to various people, Senator Magnuson of Washington called me to his table. He said, "Billy, we're having a discussion about pessimism and optimism. Are you a pessimist or an optimist?" I smiled and said, "I'm an optimist." He asked, "Why?" I said, "I've read the last page of the Bible."

The Bible speaks about a city whose builder and maker is God, where those who have been redeemed will be superior to angels. It speaks of "a pure river of water of life, clear as crystal, proceeding out of the throne of God and of the Lamb" (Revelation 22:1). It says, "And they shall see His face, and His name shall be in their foreheads. And there shall be no night there; and they need no candle, neither light of the sun; for the Lord God giveth them light: and they shall reign for ever and ever" (verses 4-5).

The next verse has a thrilling last word to say about angels: "These sayings are faithful and true: and the Lord God of the holy prophets sent His angel to shew unto His servants the things which must shortly be done" (*Angels: God's Secret Agents*, pp. 144-145, by Billy Graham).

5. Does it seem to please God to interact with angels and men? ____

Why do you say that? _____

Does God seem to interact differently with angels compared to believers? _____

Why do you say that? _____

_____

6. This study has drawn me closer to —
   ___ the angels   ___ my pastor
   ___ my Lord Jesus   ___ our church secretary

7. If you could have one wish concerning angels fulfilled right now, what would it be? _____

_____

8. How has your understanding of angels changed because of this study course? _____

_____

9. Mention several basic points from this Bible study that you feel you need to take with you into the future: _____

_____

_____

10. The story of angels will go on and on forever and ever. Some day soon you will see it unfurl before your very eyes. Amen? Yes! Amen!

Closing Prayer

Gracious Lord Jesus, we want to thank You for Your holy Word and for this Bible study. Thank You, Lord, for the angels You have sent to minister to our needs and we were unaware of it. We look forward with anticipation to seeing You come in the sky with all Your angels. We believe that our bodies will hear Your voice with the command to rise up from the dead. Give us comfort that by faith alone in Your sacrifice upon the cross we will be placed by the angels on Your right side. You have paid for our sins. You have opened the portals of heaven. You did not redeem the holy angels, but You have redeemed us. If they love and serve You the way they do, then help us to show our love and appreciation even more so. Let us learn from the angels to serve You faithfully and especially to worship You daily. The angels cannot contain themselves, but shout "hallelujah" to You. We, too, say, Hallelujah! Praise be to You! In appreciation for all You have done for us, we ask that You move us by the Spirit to feed the hungry, to clothe the naked, to visit the sick, and to do whatever we can to relieve human suffering. Especially give us grace to use our remaining time on earth to confess You openly before men that more people may come to saving faith. Hear our prayer, dear Lord. Our Father who art in heaven, hallowed be Thy name, Thy kingdom come, Thy will be done on earth as it is in heaven. Give us this day our daily bread; and forgive us our trespasses as we forgive those who trepass against us; and lead us not into temptation, but deliver us from evil. For Thine is the kingdom and the power and the glory forever and ever. Amen.

Closing Hymns

Now redemption, long expected,
See in solemn pomp appear:
All His saints, by man rejected,
Now shall meet Him in the air:
Alleluia! Alleluia! See the day of God appear.

Yes, Amen! let all adore Thee,
High on the eternal throne;
Savior, take the power and glory,
Claim the Kingdom as Your own:
Alleluia! Alleluia! Christ shall reign and Christ alone!

Praise God, from whom all blessings flow;
Praise Him, all creatures here below;
Praise Him above, ye heavenly host;
Praise Father, Son, and Holy Ghost.

The Joy of Our Future Home

ALLELUIA

The Many Wonders of Heaven

by Donald F. Ginkel

1. The Wonder of Entrance
2. The Wonder of God
3. The Wonder of the Saints
4. The Wonder of God's Family
5. The Wonder of Reward
6. The Wonder of Activity
7. The Wonder of the City

**Going to heaven is the greatest experience ever.
It boggles our minds and moves our hearts.
And it raises many challenging questions.
This seven lesson Bible study will help you find God's answers.**

A Time To Laugh... or Cry

by Donald F. Ginkel

An overview of the Old Testament. **Part 1** *(80 pages)* ten lessons from Creation in Genesis to God giving the Law in Exodus. **Part 2** *(80 pages)* from Israel conquering Canaan to Malachi's message. Each study presents an occasion for God and men to laugh and cry. The thread of the Messiah is carefully followed.

Each lesson includes a contemporary introduction with a good dose of humor, hymns, prayer, explanation of the text, probing and practical questions for discussion, plan of action, and daily Bible reading schedule. The Bible reading schedule is coordinated with the history and truths of each lesson. A 68-page Leader's Guide facilitates the teaching of the course.

To order these Bible studies and other Christian materials and a brochure call our toll free number: 1-888-772-8878